Caribou and the barren-lands

Caribou

and the barren-lands

George Calef

CANADIAN ARCTIC RESOURCES COMMITTEE, OTTAWA

FIREFLY BOOKS LIMITED, TORONTO

Canadian Cataloguing in Publication Data
Calef, George W. (George Waller), 1944-
Caribou and the barren-lands

Bibliography: p.
ISBN 0-919996-20-5, Canadian Arctic Resources Committee
0-920668-15-1, Firefly Books Ltd.

1. Caribou — Canada, Northern. 2. Caribou — Alaska. 3. Mammals — Canada, Northern. 4. Mammals — Alaska. I. Canadian Arctic Resources Committee. II. Title.

QL737.U55C34 599.73'57 C81-090063-7

The extract from I, Nuligak, *translated by Maurice Metayer, is reprinted by permission of Peter Martin Associates Ltd., copyright 1966.*

The 1977-1982 Publishing Programme of the Canadian Arctic Resources Committee is made possible by a grant from the Richard and Jean Ivey Fund.

A grant from The Canada Council assisted with the final expenses associated with George Calef's transportation, photography, and manuscript revision.

Canadian Arctic Resources Committee
46 Elgin Street, Room 11
Ottawa, Ontario, Canada
K1P 5K6

Orders to:
Firefly Books Limited
3520 Pharmacy Avenue
Scarborough, Ontario, Canada
M1W 2T8

To my parents

Beulah Waller Calef and Wesley Carr Calef

---

who taught me to see the

colours and textures of the world

The Canadian Arctic Resources Committee (CARC), founded in 1971, is an independent association of citizens promoting a balanced approach to the development of Canada's North. These people came together out of a feeling that individual citizens can make a difference – and have the responsibility to do so. They believe that there is still time to develop northern resources in a way that is rational in economic terms, in balance with the environment, and humane in its social and cultural impact.

The future of the barren-ground caribou is threatened by today's northern development pressures, population growth, hunting, and technological advances. A workable management plan for this migratory resource must be a priority of all governments. Because the participation and goodwill of Canada's native peoples are fundamental to any attempt to preserve the caribou, it is essential that there be a prompt and equitable settlement of aboriginal land claims. Only then will there be any meaningful participation of native peoples in the design and implementation of a management plan.

CARC presents this magnificent story of the barren-ground caribou at a time when discussions over an International Migratory Caribou Treaty for the Porcupine herd have broken down and the survival of other northern herds is very much in doubt. These circumstances illustrate why it is so imperative that the story of the caribou be told. *Caribou and the barren-lands* represents CARC's contribution to public understanding of this remarkable species of mammal and, it is hoped, to the survival of the caribou.

Andrew R. Thompson
Chairman, Canadian Arctic Resources Committee
1972-1980

Contents

Foreword

For the animal shall not be measured by man. In a world older and more complete than ours they move finished and complete, gifted with extensions of the senses we have lost or never attained, living by voices we shall never hear. They are not brethren, they are not underlings; they are other nations, caught with ourselves in the net of life and time, fellow prisoners of the splendour and travail of the earth.

— *Henry Beston*

If you have never seen a caribou, even from the air, you ought to apologize before attempting to write about caribou, and so I do. But you can make up for it by being suitably vicarious in the most ordinary sense — by experiencing or realizing, through imagination or sympathetic participation, the experience of another person. In *Caribou and the barren-lands,* George Calef makes that task an easy one. Through his photographs and his writing, he evokes the beauty of these animals and the majesty of the vast landscape over which they roam.

The beauty of the caribou and its homeland have long been celebrated by the Eskimo people:

Glorious it is to see
The caribou flocking down
from the forests
And beginning
Their wandering to the north.
Timidly they watch
For the pitfalls of man.
Glorious it is to see
The great herds from the forests
Spreading out over plains of white.
Glorious to see.
Yayai—ya—yiya.

Glorious it is
To see long-haired winter caribou
Returning to the forests.
Fearfully they watch
For the little people,
While the herd follows the
ebb-mark of the sea
With a storm of clattering hooves.
Glorious it is
When wandering time is come.
Yayai—ya—yiya.

Netsit, in Kenneth Brower, *Earth and the Great Weather: The Brooks Range* (San Francisco: Friends of the Earth, 1971).

But the world of the caribou is not inviolate. Indeed, the threats facing it were apparent at an early date to people such as Olaus and Mardy Murie, Robert Marshall, Sir Frank Fraser Darling, A. Starker Leopold, Lowell Sumner, George Collins, Ian McTaggart Cowan, Sigurd Olson, Ira N. Gabrielson, and Clinton Raymond ("Pink") Gutermuth. Throughout the 1950s they and many others worked to secure the designation of the Arctic National Wildlife Range in Alaska. Its nine million acres were set aside by U.S. Secretary of the Interior Fred A. Seaton in December 1960. When Secretary Seaton's successor, Stewart Udall, thought to reverse the decision, the forces of conservation were once again mobilized to dissuade him.

For decades attempts were made to seek Canada's help in a major expansion of key caribou habitat into an international Arctic Wildlife Range. The joint effort led, in October 1970, to the Arctic International Wildlife Range Conference, held in Whitehorse and chaired by Andrew Thompson. The opening paragraphs of the address by James Smith, then Commissioner of the Yukon Territory, bear repeating here: *The wildlife resources of the Arctic symbolize our common heritage. Their preservation, being a matter of deep concern to both nations, provides a challenge and hopefully an opportunity for co-operation. . . .*

There are compelling reasons which call for a global initiative to save the animals from extinction. One thing we have all learned recently is that in birth, in life and in death each species of animal and each species of plant performs innumerable functions that are crucial to the other species of life including man, and to the environment that supports all species. This complexity in the natural environment is a delicate web of relationships so that the slightest tampering with one part of the environment can have a disastrous effect on the whole. Every time we eliminate a species . . . we reduce the complexity of the systems upon which our very existence depends. Our emotional concern to save the animals from extinction is therefore a reflection of man's desire to extend his own survival on this planet.

One of the most effective efforts on behalf of the far North was achieved by Mr Justice Thomas Berger's Mackenzie Valley Pipeline Inquiry, the report of which came out in 1977. Berger advocated a wilderness park-wildlife area, to cover approximately the same area as the Canadian part of the proposed Arctic

International Wildlife Range, and to adjoin the Arctic National Wildlife Range in Alaska. The impetus given by Berger led the Canadian government in July 1978 to "freeze" all the lands north of the Porcupine River in the Yukon and to begin a process aimed at establishing a management regime for the area. Following logically from this was the need for an international treaty to protect the Porcupine caribou herd. Negotiations over such a treaty began in earnest in 1979, but have since floundered and now appear to be stalled indefinitely. The brave intentions of government to guarantee the preservation of this magnificent herd and this wilderness area are quickly being dissipated.

Defenders of the natural world cannot rest, for wilderness can be changed irrevocably. At the 1970 conference James Smith spoke of man's long and intimate association with the animal world, reminding us of the animal kingdom's rich complexities and urging us to take action to save our inheritance from extinction. He counselled our generation to recognize its international responsibility for "the wonderful, mysterious, furred and feathered creatures who share our destiny and our doom."

If it were just our own doom, that would be bad enough. But to insist on taking along with us so many of the life forms that preceded us on earth by so many eons — that insistence ought to be immensely troubling. The recently published *Global 2000 Report to the President* gives us the frightening number of species of plants and animals — from five hundred thousand to two million — that will be removed from the earth by the year 2000 *by us,* if humanity refuses to change its present habit of attacking the natural world as if there were no end to it. Looking to the Arctic and the industrial development plans for it, we can foresee that our present habit of searching for and exhausting energy resources at an increasing rate can quickly destroy the North. We face a choice. Caribou or ever more kilowatts? Whales or oil spills on troubled waters? Wilderness or wantonness with the throttle?

There are few who would suggest that arctic oil ought never to be used, but many who believe that the oil under the northern seas should be the last to be exploited, and that the exploitation should await improvements in technology and in our understanding of, and commitment to, arctic ecosystems. A great deal more needs to be learned about what arctic oil will do in arctic waters — under the ice, over the ice, on the water's surface, and, decade after decade of slow decomposition, on the sea's floor. Dynamic energy conservation and major strides in the efficiency with which we use energy can allow time for a deliberate approach to the use of the non-renewable resource of oil. And if slowing the gush of the black blood of energy should slow the speed with which we extinguish resources that will never be renewed, I hear no future generation complaining. If certain habits of growth are going to have to end sometime, why not while the earth, humanity, and caribou are still intact? One way of life does not have to die so that another can live.

Caribou and the barren-lands tells us of one of the splendid ways of life that must not die. It tells us beautifully. It reminds us that people can still take the time to seek truth from the natural world, to learn about a small but magnificent part of this planet. To have a chance to learn this truth, we had better save all the vestiges we can of the way the world was before the Industrial Revolution let us tear so much of the planet's surface apart. We ought to be brilliant enough to make do with where we've been already, trying harder to heal and less to harm.

The North is now seen to be an essential part of a place that is likewise limited — the island earth, Margaret Mead's name for it. May these pages help that island last a long time!

David Brower
Chairman, Friends of the Earth International
San Francisco

Preface

I first came to "The North" to study the caribou in early April 1971. A helicopter carried me from Whitehorse to Inuvik across a roadless wilderness that stretched for hundreds of miles in every direction. On the way we stopped briefly near several thousand caribou massed on the northernmost slopes of the Ogilvie Mountains, poised to begin the spring migration that would carry them to their calving grounds on the shores of the Arctic Ocean. It was forty-nine degrees below zero.

Despite the intense cold, the animals stood calmly grazing or resting on the snow. I was deeply impressed with the sense of their being totally at home in that landscape, of their belonging to the northern wilderness. That feeling of their oneness with the environment has grown steadily in the succeeding ten years, as I have followed the caribou over much of the Northwest Territories, the Yukon, and Alaska. Caribou have come to symbolize for me the wildness and freedom of the northland. This is my attempt to portray what I have seen and felt.

The chapters of this book are arranged by season; each opens with the story of a group of caribou during one part of the annual cycle. These narratives are intended to give a sense of the common events that recur year after year in the life of all herds of barren-ground caribou, and to evoke the changes that the march of the seasons brings to their northern homeland. The incidents portrayed are drawn from my own experiences and from the reports of fellow biologists. The second part of each chapter discusses the ecology of the caribou in a more scientific way. Here I have attempted to show how these creatures have adapted to the northern environment, and which factors play the greatest roles in determining their survival and behaviour. I have compared the details as they vary from place to place across the caribou's vast ranges.

I have called this book *Caribou and the barrenlands,* although strictly speaking the term "barrenlands" refers to only part of the caribou's range: the rocky, lake-strewn tundra of the Northwest Territories. Yet to most people's view, the country of the caribou is all barren land: harsh, unproductive, devoid of beauty. One of the purposes of these pages is to show that nothing could be further from the truth. The northern wilderness is barren only to those lacking in perception and imagination. But if we should let the great herds vanish from the barren-lands, they will indeed become what the name implies, and we will have lost a part of the majesty and mystery of life.

It is ironic that one of the joys of working in the almost uninhabited wilderness of the caribou ranges is to rediscover the importance of people. Perhaps there is some law in human affairs that the worth of individuals may be measured in inverse proportion to their numbers. In any case, I know that I count the experiences shared with others working in the North among the most valuable of my life.

I shall always be indebted to Carson Templeton and Norman Wilimovsky of the Environment Protection Board for providing me with my first opportunity to visit the Arctic and study the caribou. They started me on the path that has meant so much. Grant Lortie, who worked with me during the first three years, got me off on the right foot. I could have asked for no better teacher of the skills required to get along in the northern wilderness, and no better friend.

During my ten years of research and travels many colleagues provided valuable aid, as well as companionship and a stimulating exchange of observations and ideas about wildlife. I would like to acknowledge Rod Boertje, Tony Bubenik, Ray Cameron, Bob Decker, Rick Farnell, the late Don Gill, Vern Hawley, Doug Heard, Jim Hemming, Ben Hubert, Roy Jacobson, Peggy Kuropat, Bob Le Resche, Art Martell, Bob McKillop, Frank Miller, Art Pearson, Dan Roby, Dave Roseneau, Don Russell, John Russell, and Bob Stephenson.

The Alaska Department of Fish and Game, Canadian Wildlife Service, Northwest Territories Wildlife Service, U.S. Fish and Wildlife Service, and Yukon

Wildlife Branch all offered me co-operation and assistance during my research and photography, and I am much indebted.

Research in the northern wilderness depends heavily on transportation by aircraft — a skilful and co-operative pilot can make the difference between the success and failure of a project. I have been lucky to fly with some of the best: Dunc Bell, Bob Cameron, Mark Crossman, Dennis Hosking, Paul Jones, Willie Laeserich, Wynn Muff, Frank O'Connor, and Ivan Rand.

All ideas and aspirations need a catalyst to start them towards realization. Before I started this book, I was approached by Kit Vincent to work with him on another project. When I replied that I was thinking about doing a book on caribou, he told me that I'd better quit thinking about it and get busy writing. He convinced the Canadian Arctic Resources Committee to sponsor the project and he maintained a continuing interest in it. For his encouragement from beginning to end I am grateful.

As the manuscript took shape, I received helpful comments and criticism from many colleagues. I wish to thank the following friends who each read one or more chapters and offered valuable advice in their areas of expertise: John Bayly, Margaret Cook, Bob Decker, Doug Heard, Ben Hubert, Bob Janes, Ernie Kuyt, Don Miller, Frank Miller, Ray Schweinsburg, Bob Stephenson, and Don Thomas. I particularly want to thank Jim Davis of the Alaska Department of Fish and Game. He gave freely of his time and knowledge of the caribou in helping me plan and carry out the trips in Alaska. His personal interest contributed tremendously to the success of this project. He also provided me with the most recent data on the Alaskan herds.

I thank Al Hochbaum for his guidance and encouragement during my writing. A seasoned author who knows well the conflict between the long hours required at the desk and the lure of the landscape, he gave me practical suggestions for getting the job done. His wise counsel at two or three critical turning points saved me from making mistakes that would have jeopardized the project. He even tipped me off about where to go to get some of my best photographs.

Tom Bergerud of the University of Victoria read the entire draft manuscript and offered dozens of valuable suggestions for its improvement. I also drew heavily on his many publications to supplement my own observations. Tom knows more about caribou than anyone else in the world. I feel privileged to have had his advice and friendship during my research on caribou and in writing this book.

This book was sponsored and financed by the Canadian Arctic Resources Committee. I thank Murray Coolican, the executive director, for his support of the project during its two-and-a-half year span. The Canadian Arctic Resources Committee not only funded me during the writing, but also subsidized two field seasons during which I obtained most of the photographs required to portray the life cycle of the caribou. They also provided editorial services. Without this assistance, and that of The Canada Council, the book could never have been produced.

Edie Van Alstine directed the entire project and managed the production of the book. She raised vital funds, negotiated all arrangements with designers, printers, and the co-publisher, and oversaw the final production, distribution, and promotion. She spared no effort to make this book the best it could possibly be. At times I think she believed in it more than I did, and I am grateful for all her work.

Janet Wright, the editor, deserves great credit for helping transform my manuscripts into a book. The time and effort she devoted to the project went far beyond the requirements of her job. I thank her for her patience and cheerfulness during the final series of deadlines; she made a gruelling schedule bearable.

Above all, I thank Mary-Lee Broderick for sticking it out through all the ups and downs of the project. She shared not only the joys but also the disappointments and frustrations of the field work and the writing without ever losing her enthusiasm and confidence in this venture to tell the story of the caribou.

Prologue

Caribou are the deer of the North. Shaped by the snows of millennia, they are completely at home in the country of winter. Theirs are the lands so recently emerged from beneath the snow and glaciers of the great ice age: the windswept tundra, the "land of little sticks" where the stunted trees of the boreal forest cease their northward march, the ice-hung cordilleras. Over these meagre lands they travel, obeying the commands of the seasons: the melting of snow, the budding of plants, the hatching of mosquitoes, the freeze-up of lakes and rivers. Like the wind that passes over the tundra wilderness and is gone, caribou are forever on the move. They appear on one distant horizon and vanish on the other. And it is their comings and goings that set the cadence of life on the barren-lands.

This is the story of the great herds of barren-ground caribou and their yearly migrations through northern Canada and Alaska. The massing of the bison has vanished from the plains; the vast flocks of passenger pigeons that once darkened the sky are gone, never to return. But the majestic herds of caribou move over the tundra today as they always have, submerging the harsh land beneath a tide of life.

To follow the caribou is to experience every facet of the northern environment, for the caribou are the central creatures of the North, the pulse of life in the land. They quicken the country not merely by adding animation and excitement themselves, but also by carrying along a host of other creatures: the wolf, the fox, the raven. The empty tundra may appear a drab and barren place, but let one caribou trot onto the skyline of an esker and the land comes alive. These pages record the drama that may still be witnessed today — by following the caribou.

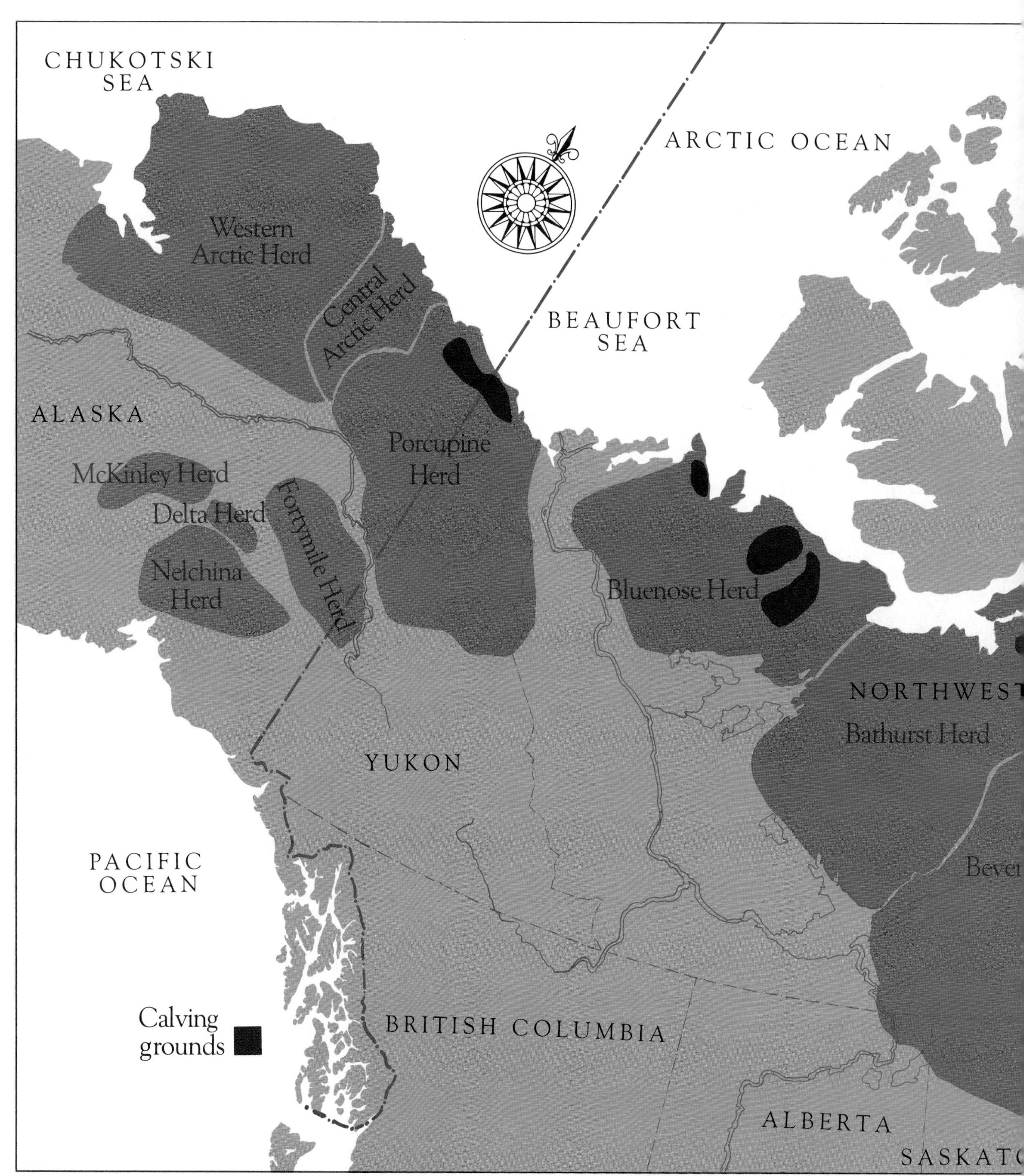

Major barren-ground caribou herds of Canada and selected Alaskan herds

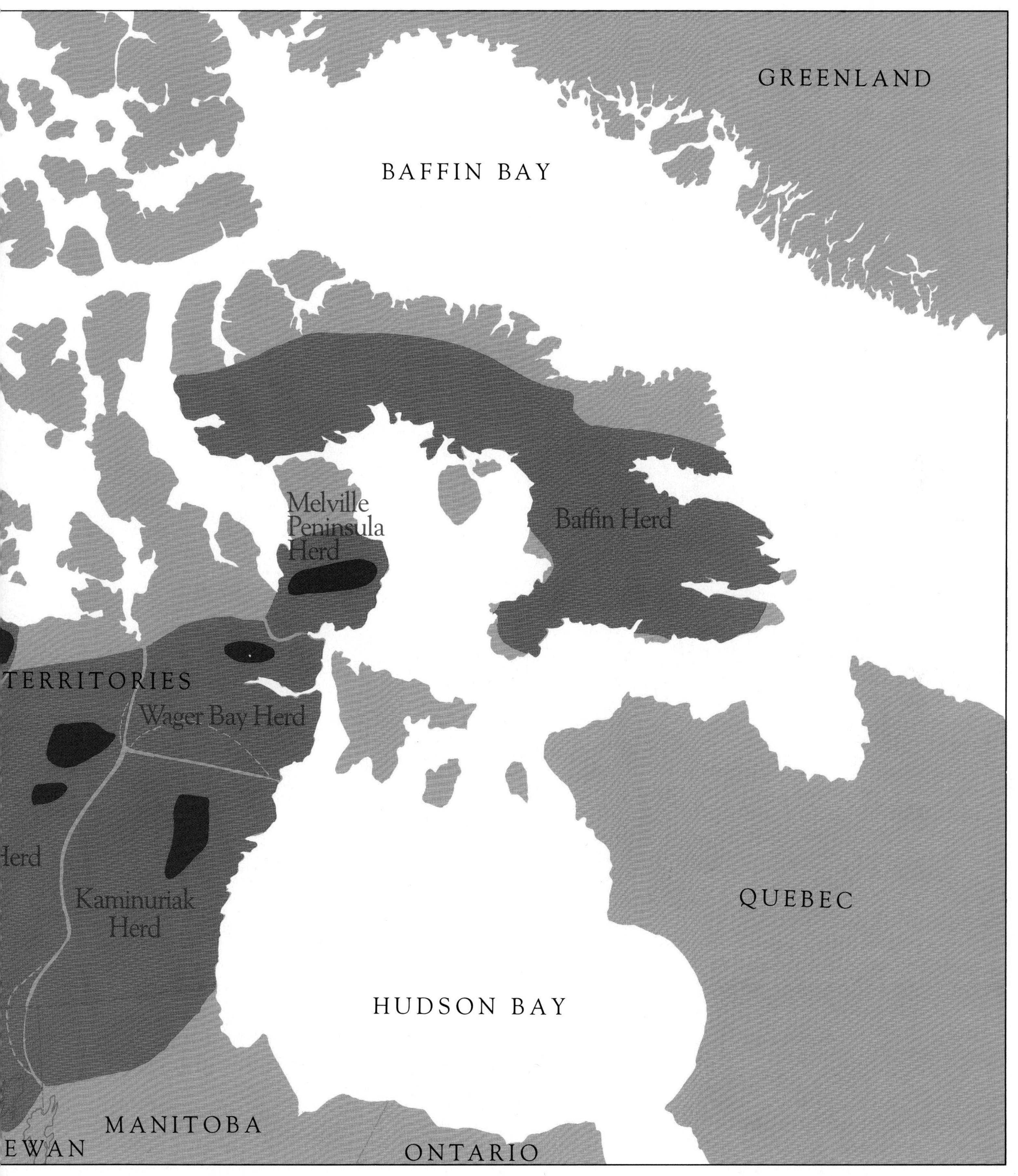
GREENLAND
BAFFIN BAY
Melville
Peninsula
Herd
Baffin Herd
TERRITORIES
Wager Bay Herd
Herd
Kaminuriak
Herd
QUEBEC
HUDSON BAY
MANITOBA
EWAN
ONTARIO

Part I

A year of life on the barren-lands

Spring
The river of life

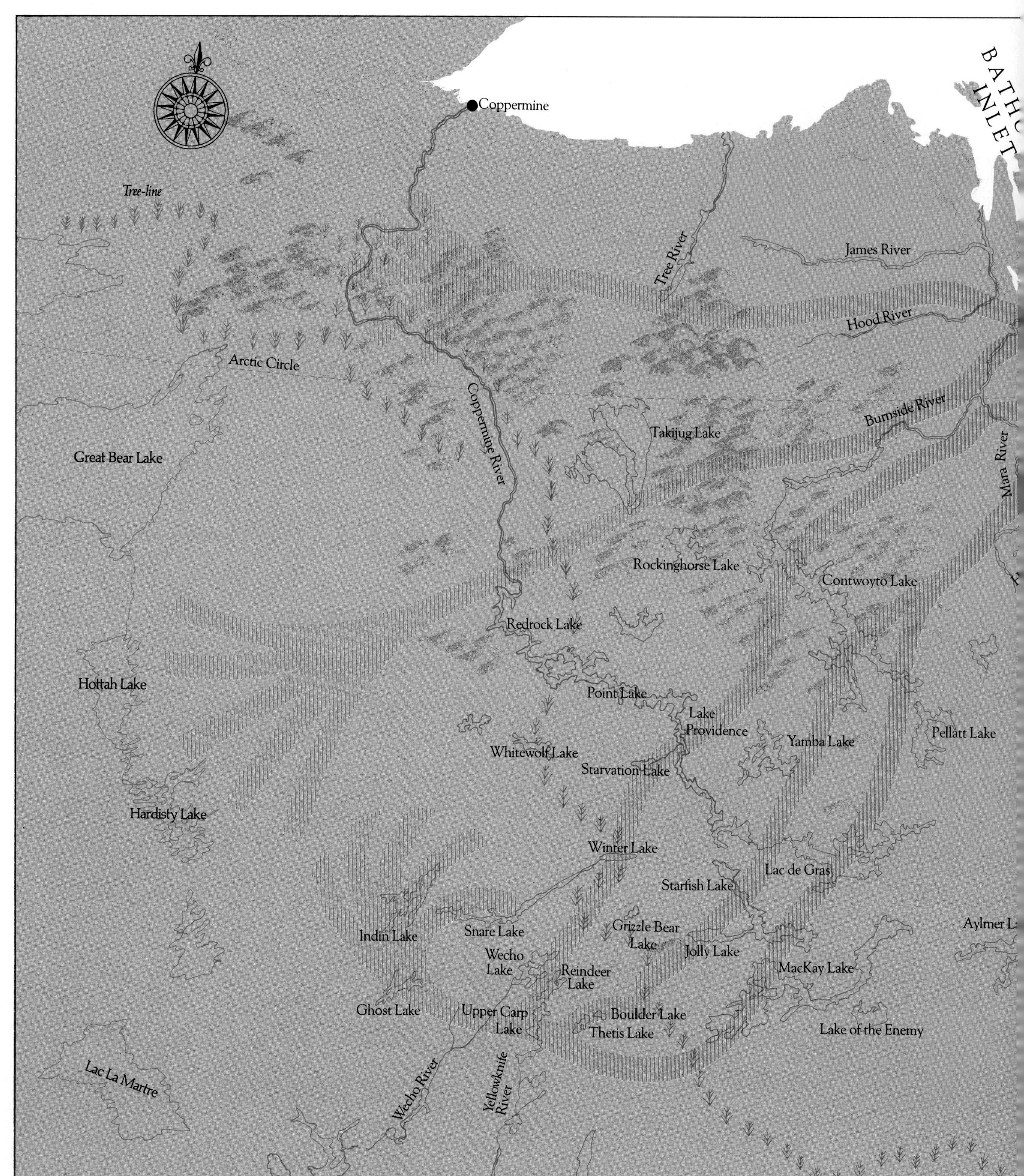

A spring migration of the Bathurst herd

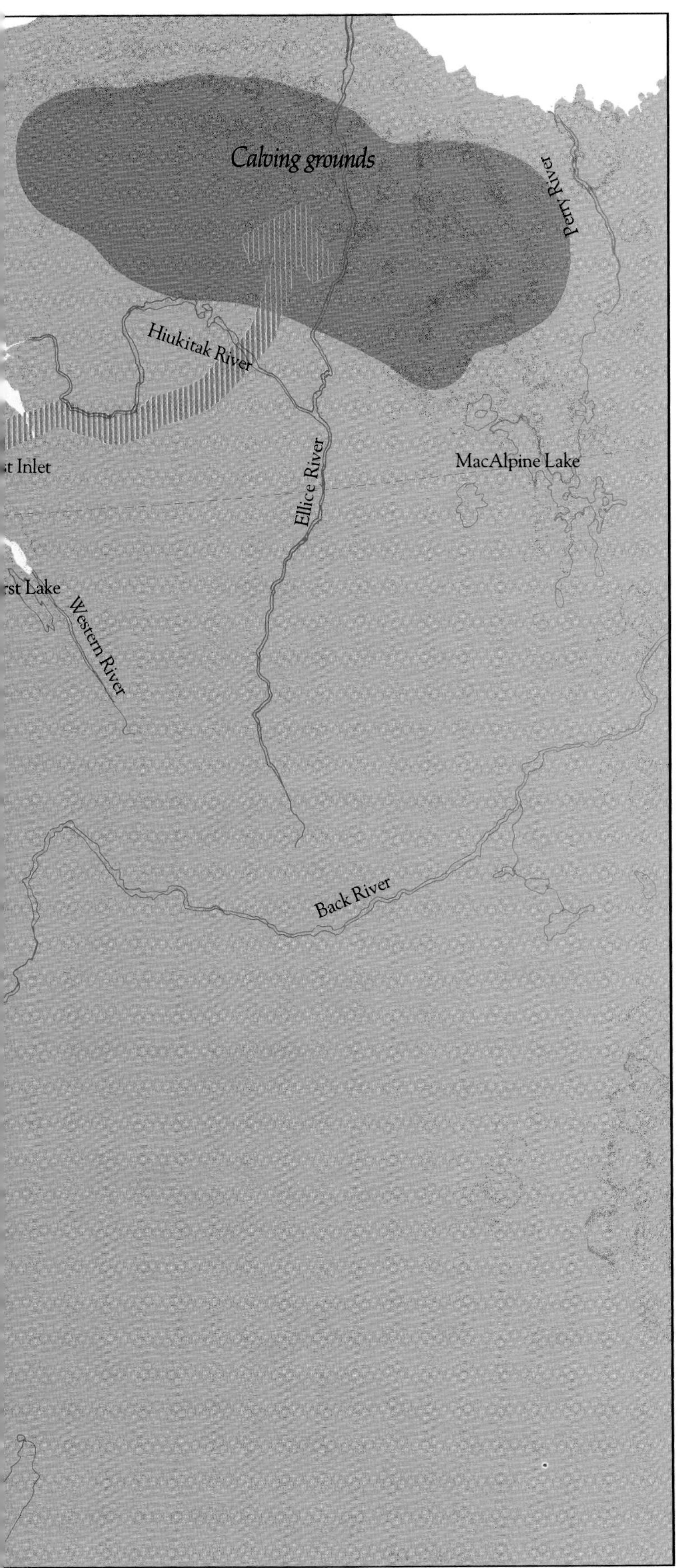

Every kind of country is perfect for something, even the harsh, spare land along the northern tree-line, where the straggly spruce of the boreal forest give way to the windswept immensity of the barren-lands. The scenery cannot be called spectacular. The land is largely flat, the trees few and stunted. Beyond these last vestiges of the forest, the frozen tundra stretches away so featureless beneath the drifts that, even from an airplane, it is impossible to tell where the land ends and the lakes begin. In the grip of ice and snow the country appears empty and lifeless.

But here, when the lengthening days of April portend the defeat of another winter, this seemingly bleak country is the setting for one of the earth's great wildlife spectacles. For the barren-lands are the country of the caribou. Each spring the migrations of the vast herds repeat, symbolically, the renewal of life on the barren-lands, as when this country first emerged from beneath the great glaciers of the ice age.

Like all renewals, it begins almost imperceptibly. Who can say when the caribou's dull endurance of winter gives way to their relentless urge to travel? But when the long blue shadows lie on the snows of spring, a restlessness seizes the small bands of caribou as they lie on the frozen lakes or bare mountain ridges where they have spent the winter. Cows lead their almost-year-old calves into the company of others. Yearlings and young bulls fall into line. Scattered tracks in the snow become paths. Paths converge to become deep trails. Long files of caribou form, mysteriously orienting in the age-old directions that generations have followed before. The river of life begins to flow once again.

The restlessness of spring affects the caribou of the Western Arctic herd on the bare ridges and forested valleys in Alaska's Brooks Range. Along the Blackstone, Wind, and Bonnet Plume rivers of the Yukon, the cows of the Porcupine herd sense the change. On Ghost Lake, Drybones Lake, and Lake of the Enemy, the animals of the Bathurst herd feel it. Half the world away, in Siberia and Scandinavia, the urge of spring seizes the wild reindeer. And so, like the others of her kind, the old cow crossing the rocky hills above Boulder Lake was setting out on the journey that, each year, takes her herd across hundreds of miles of forest and tundra to their calving grounds near Bathurst Inlet.

The old cow led some three hundred other caribou over the divide separating Boulder Lake from Thetis Lake. Her wide, sharp-edged hooves felt for footing on the broken and uneven rocks, as she picked her way down the snow-covered bluff. The wind played with the animals' manes as they passed slowly along, heads down, silhouetted against the evening glow.

These caribou had been drifting gradually eastward for well over a month. During the bitter cold of February they had travelled slowly, no more than a mile or two a day — across Ghost Lake, then past the Wecho River. Daytime temperatures rarely crept above thirty below. The sun shone huge and red through the ice fog. At night it fell to minus forty or lower. Then in early March the weather had warmed and the caribou had picked up their pace. The spring migration was underway.

The old cow and her band were the head of the migration, the first to reach Boulder Lake. In their wake thirty thousand barren-ground caribou of the Bathurst herd were strung out for fifty miles or more along the migration trail. On the hundreds of lakes scattered among the scrubby spruce forest, groups like hers were bedding down, each animal pawing out a shallow bed, then bending its front legs to drop to the snow and curl up. The caribou settled well out in the open, away from the trees — a precaution against the wolves that haunted the herd.

The next morning they started down Boulder Lake. Their route across the lake ended in a bay at the mouth of the Surprise River. Here the old cow and her band fed as they pushed a path through the forest to the next lake half a mile away.

As always when they travelled, the animals kept as much as possible to the firm footing of wind-packed lakes and rivers. They left the ice only to feed or when they had to get from one lake to the next. In this way they avoided the soft, energy-sapping snow that lay among the trees.

For the next few miles of their journey they followed the river through a series of lakes connected by stretches of rapids. Despite the cold, the swift water remained open, sending up steam that covered the nearby trees with rime. Thin ice lurked several hundred yards below each open stretch. Here the caribou kept close to shore where the ice was thicker, or left the river briefly. They halted for the night on a big lake above the chain of rapids.

That night the temperature dropped and the wind picked up. As the caribou lay curled in the snow, there were deep booms and groans from the ice beneath them shuddering in contraction. With the onset of cold again, the leading animals did not move on. But those behind continued to pour onto the lake over the next few days. Scores of migrating bands piled up here. Groups ranging from ten or twenty to a hundred times that many dotted the surface of the lake. At all hours of the day or night lines of caribou trailed on and off the ice, going to and from feeding areas. Trails criss-crossed the lake in mazes.

In dawn's half-light a long mournful chorus of howls floated in the still air. The notes rose and fell, blended together, and trembled away. Eight wolves grouped together on the ice near a small island, their tails waving slowly with excitement as they sang. Two almost-full-grown pups danced around their mother, nuzzling their faces against hers. Ghostly and quavering with distance, the call of an answering pack returned from the forest. The two bands of hunters howled back and forth for several minutes before the last notes drifted into silence.

The wolves had arrived with the caribou. As the migrating bands had funnelled together along the Surprise River, the hundreds of wolves that had been shadowing the scattered caribou all winter also concentrated here. Their ominous tracks, as big as a man's hand, mingled with the hoof-prints of their prey. These wolves would stay with the migration for weeks to come.

Their howl completed, the wolves lay down near the island. A creamy white male, weighing over a hundred pounds with his belly full, curled up beside a silvery grey bitch. She was in heat and her mate was sticking close by. The energetic pups had a wrestle, growling and biting playfully at one another's head and neck, each trying to tumble his foe.

Three ravens came flapping out of the sunrise. They flared over the dark stain of the pack's kill from the night before, their wings wheezing in the stillness. Then one raven uttered a clear bell-like note and they glided down. The pups stopped their play to eye the birds as they strutted and flapped around the remains of the caribou, squabbling over the pickings that the wolves had missed.

Soon one pup found the antics of the birds too tempting. He raced out, scattering the scavengers, and began poking around the pieces of hide and scattered hair, his nose quivering. He finally settled for a partially chewed shoulder blade, which he carried away from the area trampled by the pack's feeding. There his paws worked quickly, sending up a shower of snow as he hid his prize. Then he trotted back to the pack.

For most of the morning the adult wolves lazed conten-

tedly, all but the big male. He got up restlessly several times to frisk about in front of his mate, trying to stir up a response. Each time she rose to stretch and urinate the big male was there, prancing excitedly behind her and waving his fluffy tail. He sniffed her sign, then marked the spots himself, scratching up the area stiff-leggedly afterwards. A tawny grey male also followed the pair, hanging back about fifteen feet behind the larger male. Twice the white wolf whirled on him. The grey rolled on his back in submission, fawning as the dominant animal stood over him.

In the afternoon the female began to play with her mate. The pair rubbed side by side, licked faces, and romped together. Several times he mounted her for a few seconds, only to slide off again. The tawny male followed, but always at a distance. The dominant animal regularly confronted him, forcing him to roll on his back or side in submission. At last in mid-afternoon the bitch received her mate. They remained tied together for several minutes, facing in opposite directions. The tawny grey watched intently as he lay a few yards away, but made no move to interfere; the other wolves paid no attention.

When only a clear glow remained in the evening sky, the wolves rose and stretched. They gathered for the ritual of another howl before trotting off down the shoreline, the creamy male in the lead. The pack paralleled the shore for a mile and a half to a small point. Here a young female dropped behind, hiding among the dark shadows of the spruce. The other seven hunters crossed the point and continued into the bay.

Most of the caribou had come out of the forest following their afternoon feeding; bands lay resting all over the lake. The wolves fanned out across the ice towards the nearest group. One of the caribou glimpsed them when they were about three hundred yards away. She stared carefully for a second or two, making sure that she had seen something, and then stood up quickly, facing the intruders. Her actions alerted her neighbours, who jumped to their feet facing in the same direction. As the wolves came on, several of the caribou assumed the alarm posture, cocking one hind leg to the side, heads high and alert. A few urinated. Nervousness spread through the band. More caribou got up. Now the wolves loped forward: their intent was clear. The caribou bolted in an explosion of flying snow, bunching tightly as they fled. The wolves lunged in pursuit, huge paws spreading to grip the snow, but the caribou easily stayed ahead. The wolves swung to head the band towards the ambush.

As the fleeing caribou raced towards her hiding place, the young female wolf tensed, gathering her long legs under her. When the caribou passed a hundred yards away, she darted out.

The lead caribou saw her charge and swerved towards the safety of the open lake where they could take advantage of their speed. But as the band swung around behind the leaders, the old cow's calf turned wide and separated from the group. Instantly the lone wolf locked all her attention on it. With a burst of speed she closed the distance slightly. Then as the calf headed back towards the other caribou, the bitch cut across its arc of travel and drew alongside. Her powerful jaws snapped on the calf's muzzle, and the two skidded and slewed across the snow. The calf jerked spasmodically in a desperate effort to shake off the attacker, but the wolf's grip was solid. The doomed animal's struggle was already weakening when the great white male arrived to end the hunt with one crushing bite to the back of its skull.

As the wolves stood panting beside their kill, breaths streaming in the cold, the caribou slowed, then stopped. They walked for half a mile, nervously looking back over their shoulders now and again. The caribou worked off their anxiety with small acts of aggression. Some threatened others close by with their antlers. One cow mounted the one ahead of her and rode the startled animal for a few steps as it spurted ahead. At last they lay down again.

The old cow gave no outward sign that she noticed her calf was missing. She did not search for him as she would have done the previous summer. The bond tying her to the calf had weakened naturally over the winter. In a few weeks more she would have had to chase him off to make way for her new one. During the winter the calf had been the one maintaining their bond. He was the one who followed her when she went to feed, rather than she calling him as during his infancy; he who watched her for cues at the first sign of danger; and he who tried to stay close by when she fled, but this time not close enough.

The big male wolf ripped open the body cavity of the calf and began to devour the liver. As he pushed his head inside, the dark fresh blood stained the fur on his face and ruff. His mate tore at the throat and head, seeking the fat-rich tongue. The other animals moved in to share the feast. This made the fourth caribou that the pack had killed in the past week. Although the wolves were in prime condition with perhaps an inch of fat on their rumps, they still ate whenever they could kill. The pack fed peaceably except for an occasional growl of warning

from one of the dominant animals. Their powerful jaws splintered the leg bones to obtain the fatty marrow. Even the skull was crushed for the brains. When they were satisfied, the wolves withdrew one by one and rested. An arctic fox trotting across the ice caught the smell of the fresh kill. Homing in upwind, he cautiously loped towards the carcass, leaving a straight line of round tracks in the snow. The dozens of kills on this lake were providing him with a rich feeding ground.

After several days the weather warmed again; the snow thawed and began to settle. Caribou were leaving the lake. The old cow fell into line as her band left early after noon, following the tracks of those that had already departed. They continued up the Surprise River for eight miles, stopping on the next big lake. In the morning they turned straight north up a long narrow lake connecting with the river. The trees here were small and stunted, scarcely deserving of the name, though they had grown for a hundred summers to attain their few feet of wind-twisted height. With each mile the caribou travelled north, the forest thinned out more. By evening only a few spindly trees clung here and there on the rocky ridges, stark against the gold sky.

Then the trees vanished. The world had simplified to barest essentials: snow, rock, and sky. The caribou had reached the barren-lands. It was the last day of March.

Now that the caribou had left the trees, it was no longer so important for them to travel on the lakes. Everywhere the unimpeded wind had blasted the snow to a rock-like consistency. Even the drifts were hard enough to support the animals' weight. Thus, when the travellers departed next morning, they struck a course approximately thirty-five degrees east of north. For the next six weeks they would scarcely deviate from this heading, which would carry them three hundred and fifty miles across the winter emptiness of the barren-lands.

Behind the vanguard that had gained the tundra, the hundreds of caribou bands comprising the main migration were threading their way through the forest by several different routes. Most took the path used by the old cow, but some followed the McCrea River straight east, finally hitting the barrens just north of Drybones Lake. Others went north through Upper Carp Lake, into Reindeer Lake and beyond, up the Yellowknife River. As each stream of migrants reached the country beyond the trees, they set their course towards Bathurst Inlet.

The long lines of caribou all but vanished into the immensity of the barren-lands. Their pale coats blended with the grey and white of the landscape. A group resting among the scattered rocks on a ridge top appeared as just so many stones. On the compacted snow the caribou's broad, round hooves left little impression. The wind, endlessly shifting the fine snow, soon obliterated their tracks and the shallow craters they dug to feed on the sparse lichens. And so the caribou moved on, leaving little sign of their passing in the world of rock and snow.

It took the old cow and her band only a week to reach Jolly Lake, some thirty miles northeast. They travelled down the long esker that runs into the south shore. This rounded ridge of sand and gravel offered both easy travelling and a familiar landmark.

The great esker was well known to not only the caribou. The grey wolf bitch led her mate down its slope to a sandy, willow-covered flat near a small lake. Side by side they sniffed the snow for the dozen entrances to the complex den that they had used here the previous year. Their tails wagged as they explored the familiar smells. That afternoon, while the male sunned on a rise nearby, the female began to dig out the packed snow and fallen soil blocking the mouth of one of the passages. In these sandy tunnels she would give birth to her pups at the end of May. For the next month the pair would hunt far and wide as the caribou migration moved through.

The lengthening days of April passed quickly as the old cow's band pushed on with their journey. They reached the west end of Starfish Lake, fifteen miles further north, two days after crossing Jolly. Three days later the caribou splashed through the overflow on the blue ice of the Coppermine River, a few miles downstream from the huge frozen expanse of Lac de Gras. Soon after passing the Coppermine they joined two other bands, bringing the group's strength to over a thousand animals. As the long file travelled slowly along the ridges, dwarfed against the lingering twilight in the vast sky vault of the barren-lands, there was an inexorability in their movement. Theirs was the purposefulness, the urge of all life, to survive and multiply, to fill every corner of the earth no matter how bleak and inhospitable.

Day by day the caribou steadily covered the miles towards their distant goal. Their gait, though appearing unhurried, ate up the ground. Scarcely had they made their appearance on one horizon before they were specks vanishing in the distance. One long bright day passed much the same as the next; there was little variation in the rhythm of

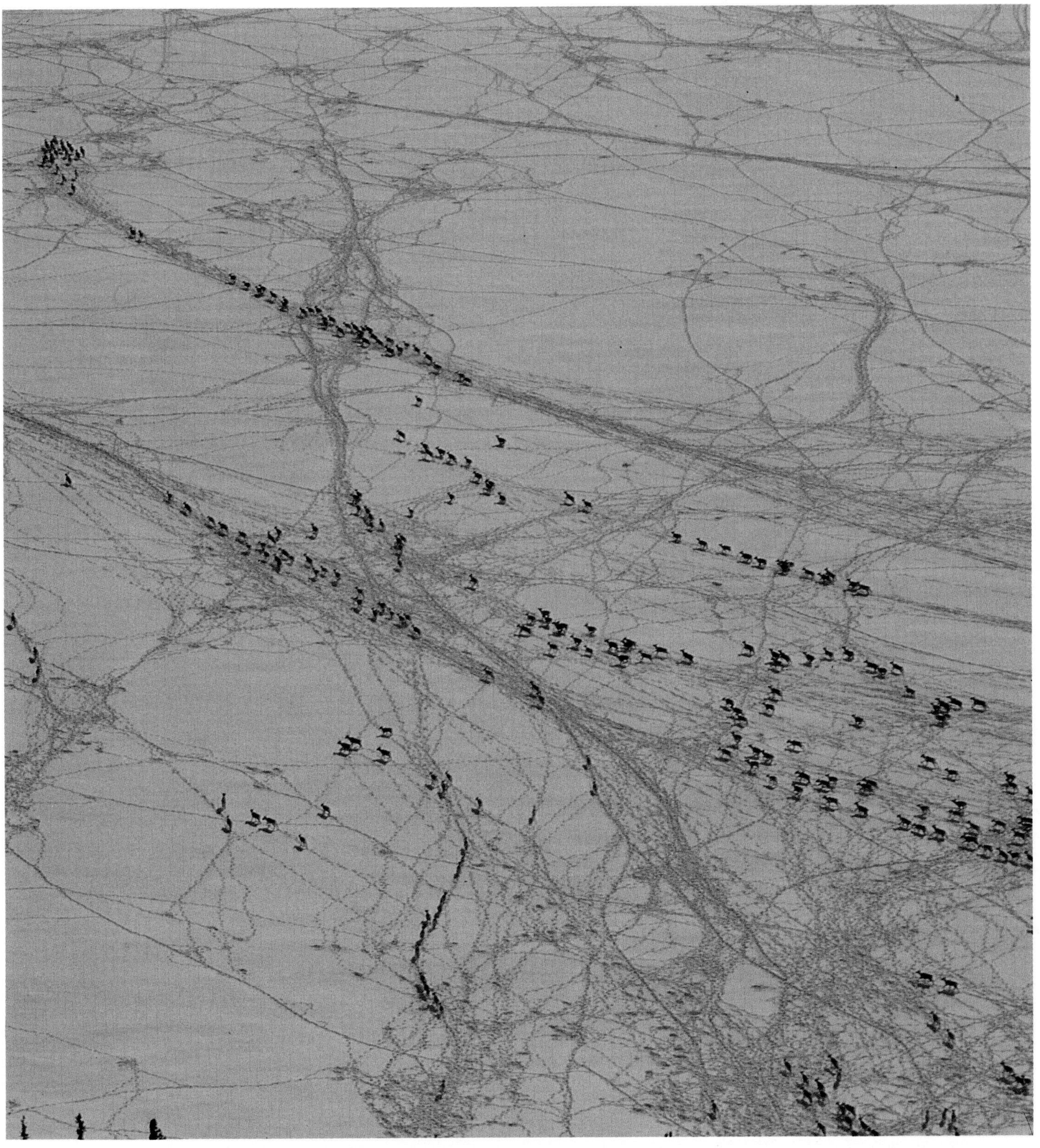

travel among the hundreds of bands making up the flow of migration. The particular events that befell each individual or band mattered little. The caribou were but a part of the larger pageant, unfolding as it had for a thousand springs and more.

Yamba Lake was the next landmark. Then they found their way through the lake-littered country beyond, and on the twentieth of April the long stretch of Contwoyto Lake came into sight. They crossed the ice to feed on an island in the middle of the lake. Here stood a weather station: a couple of small buildings, the inevitable rows of fuel drums buried in the snow, and a tall radio tower. This tiny outpost was the only speck of human habitation in all the hundreds of miles between Yellowknife and Bathurst Inlet. A figure appeared from the drifted-over weather shack, looked around, and hurried back inside. He emerged a moment later with a companion, pointing to the herd. Some of the animals stopped feeding to stare as the men walked forward. A few took the alarm posture. But when the humans halted and merely stood watching, the caribou resumed grazing. The two men stood in the wind, looking for a while, then went inside.

Now the temperature sometimes rose above freezing. Bare spots mottled the ridges, and the caribou fed on the plants exposed there. Flocks of snow buntings, arriving from the South, shared these openings with the caribou. They flew from patch to patch like snowflakes in the wind, snapping up seeds and berries that remained from the autumn crop.

Once past Contwoyto the caribou continued northeast to hit the Mara River. Then their course roughly paralleled the Mara to its junction with the Hackett. From there they struck northeast again, crossing the rugged hills west of Bathurst Inlet. Most of the young bulls had dropped behind in the past two weeks, as had many of the barren cows. There were also fewer calves still following their mothers; the wolves had continued to take their toll, and other calves had simply lagged behind.

It was now May. Life was returning to the land. Many south slopes were bare, and for the first time in seven months the caribou could feed without pawing through snow. Streams showed dark open patches; water trickled across the ice. Geese coursed over the tundra, their wild calls of homecoming carrying away on the wind.

The old cow stood looking down the rough brown hills to the ice of Bathurst Inlet. Her journey was almost over. The calving grounds lay only seventy-five miles away, a week's travel, no more. Her calf had not survived this time. But the old cow had made this journey many times before. Perhaps some of the caribou crossing the ice below were her descendants. And she would come this way again each spring as long as she lived, sometimes leading a calf successfully, sometimes failing. Even now, new life was stirring within her. The cows that had travelled with her were filing down the slope. The old cow lowered her head and stepped into line.

In a life of movement, the spring migration is the caribou's most urgent journey; for it carries the cows, heavy with the promise of new life, from their winter ranges to the distant tundra or mountains where the new generation is born. During this trek, which may cover hundreds of miles and take two months to complete, the caribou encounter virtually every hazard of the northern environment: the heavy, sodden snows of spring, barriers of ice-choked and flooded rivers, the attacks of wolves, and the onslaught of blizzards as the wind screams unbroken over the barren-lands.

It seems a misnomer to call the movement from the winter ranges to the calving grounds the "spring" migration. Spring it may be by the calendar, but the conditions faced by the caribou as they travel would be considered winter anywhere but in the far North. When the caribou begin their migration in March or April, the lakes and streams are frozen, the plants are frozen, the land itself is frozen. Even in April temperatures may still fall to -40° F. Storms sweep the land.

Exactly what starts the animals on their way remains something of a mystery. Why does the migration begin in mid-March one year and not until late April the next? Why do the caribou on one winter range start north, while a group 200 miles away delays for several weeks, even though they may have further to travel to the calving grounds? Obviously the animals do not set their schedules by the calendar. The increasing daylight following the long dark winter likely has a physiological effect, predisposing the animals to migration. Such physiological changes have been well documented in studies of migratory birds. Although similar research is lacking for caribou, the same principles probably apply. Certainly the bands become more restless and gather together in larger groups as the days lengthen in late winter.

Changes in the snow cover seem to be the final stimulus that starts the spring movement. On some caribou ranges the snow may be melting away and some new plant growth starting before the migration begins. Such conditions often prevail in interior Alaska and in Newfoundland. On the ranges of the barren-ground caribou in central Canada, the changes take place more subtly. There snow usually still covers the ground when the migration begins, but the increasing solar radiation causes settling and the formation of "suncrusts." The snow becomes more difficult for the caribou to dig through in their search for food, and heavier to push aside while travelling. The caribou react by moving. Once they start, snowstorms or intense cold may halt their progress for a while, but as soon as suitable weather returns they continue their journey.

When spring thaws come late, the caribou delay their start. A month or more may separate the earliest and latest dates that a particular caribou herd starts its migration. If the trek begins late, the animals must travel faster to reach the calving grounds before giving birth. Rates of travel of fifteen to twenty miles per day are not unusual if the pregnant cows approach the calving grounds behind schedule. Occasionally bad weather delays them so long that they find themselves in a race with time, covering up to forty miles a day in a dash to reach the traditional calving place.

During the migration the caribou seek routes on which the snow is shallow or has melted, blown away, or formed a crust hard enough to support them. This preference accounts for the caribou's use of the wind-packed surfaces of frozen lakes and rivers in the boreal forest of central Canada. In the Yukon and Alaska lakes are scarcer; there the preferred routes lie on mountain ridges where the wind compacts or blows away the snow, making both travelling and feeding easier.

Through thousands of years of life in the North, the caribou's behaviour has evolved to make them efficient travellers in the snow. They move in single file, each animal stepping in the tracks of the one before it. Sometimes hundreds or even thousands of animals pass over a single trail, compacting the snow almost through to bare ground. But even if only a few animals travel one behind the other, they save considerable energy. If another group later uses the trail, they have the advantage not only of decreased depth, but also of a harder surface resulting from the snow recrystallizing.

So ingrained is the caribou's instinct for seeking the routes of least resistance that they will follow any disturbance in the snow that offers easier travelling. Migrating animals will travel along seismic lines and snow roads. Each year collisions with trains and cars kill hundreds of wild and domestic reindeer in Scandinavia. Caribou even use snowmobile trails; biologists have used such devices to direct migrating caribou into traps to capture them for marking. I once even had caribou follow my snowshoe trail right into camp.

Because caribou do not always winter on the same ranges and in the same numbers each year, the pattern of spring migration varies from time to time and among different herds. Sometimes most of the caribou from a herd winter in one place and come together early in the spring to move off in one great exodus. Then the migration proceeds along a single wide front. In the spring of 1978 I witnessed such a migration of the Beverly herd. Virtually all of the females and immature animals moved off together from their winter ranges along the Alberta-Northwest Territories border, leaving behind them a fifty-mile-wide swath through the land in which hardly a patch of snow remained untrampled. One hundred thousand caribou travelled the 400 miles to the calving grounds in essentially one corridor.

On the other hand, caribou from one herd often winter on several widely separated ranges. These groups start on their way at different times, and the migration then proceeds by a variety of routes. Small streams of migrants come together into larger and larger channels. These may again divide, separate for a time, then flow together once more. A map of such a migration path looks like the channel of a braided river system. Such a pattern has characterized the migrations that I have followed while studying the Porcupine herd. The caribou herds in Alaska whose winter ranges are scattered through mountainous terrain also generally follow this pattern.

The winter ranges may be so far apart that caribou from each area pursue completely separate paths to their common goal. For

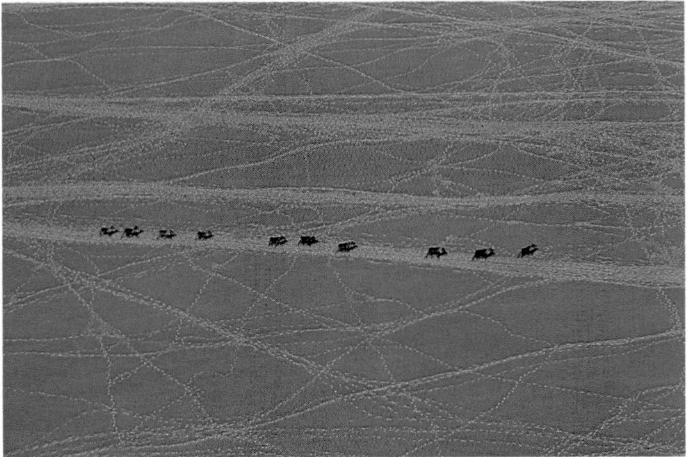

instance, members of the Bathurst herd that winter near Great Slave Lake travel almost straight north to reach the calving grounds east of Bathurst Inlet. Another group commonly wintering near Great Bear Lake travels east-northeast. A third major part of the population often winters on the tundra near the community of Coppermine. This group heads straight east, or even slightly southeast to reach the same destination.

Pregnant females lead the spring migration; those that will calve first arrive earliest on the calving grounds. Most of the previous year's calves follow their mothers, thus gaining experience in the route and pattern of migration. Some of these calves, however, especially the males, may leave their mothers during the later stages of migration and never travel all the way to the calving grounds. Early in the migration the barren cows and juvenile males (two- and three-year-old animals) travel with the pregnant cows and calves; but these non-productive animals, especially the young bulls, also usually drop out of the migration somewhere before the calving grounds. Mature males rarely migrate with the females, but instead remain on the winter ranges for several weeks after the cows depart. They travel later at a more leisurely pace, often waiting until the snow melts, exposing the vegetation. They do not see the cows again until they rejoin the great herds in mid-summer.

Caribou apparently have to learn to migrate. If calves do not participate in one annual cycle of travel with the herd, their drive to migrate does not develop. Experience with re-introducing caribou to areas from which they were extirpated by hunting has shown that if adults from migratory herds are placed into a new range they disperse, usually vanishing forever from the new site. The only successful introductions of migratory caribou have been on remote islands from which the animals could not escape. However, young calves captured before they have made their first cycle of migration will stay put if they are moved to the new location in the absence of adults. In Sweden abnormal behaviour resulted when domestic reindeer were transported by truck from their summer pastures to winter ranges, rather than being herded on an autumn migration, as was traditional. The following spring many reindeer did not return to their summer pastures in the mountains. Their failure to return probably resulted from the large number of inexperienced animals, and possibly also from the lack of reinforcement of the migratory behaviour among those that had migrated previously.

Caribou do not simply move north onto the tundra. Rather, they return to specific places each spring to bear their calves. The way that caribou find their way back to one small area across hundreds of miles of tundra remains a mystery, like the navigational abilities of so many animal travellers. Do the calves learn the way by following their mothers? Is the migration led by experienced leaders who have learned the route being followed? Do leaders change when one route is used rather than another? Can caribou navigate using the stars or by magnetic orientation, as has been discovered in birds? These questions remain unanswered.

It has been suggested that the caribou could reach their calving grounds merely by following topographical routes of least resistance such as watersheds, heights of land, or mountain ranges. Indeed, many of the traditional routes do have these obvious features. If so, then learning must be involved for the caribou to know which features to follow, for there are always alternative routes that could carry the animals away from the correct line of travel. For example, one of the major spring migration routes of the Bathurst herd crosses Contwoyto Lake, which runs at right angles to the line of travel. If the caribou blindly followed only the path of least resistance, they should

turn aside here, following the smooth ice of the lake rather than crossing directly as they do. On many routes eskers run perpendicular to the routes of travel, offering invitingly easy passage; but the caribou ignore these. New features on the landscape, such as roads or seismic lines, are used only when they run roughly in the direction the caribou want to travel.

Perhaps the best evidence that caribou can orient accurately comes from the spring movements of Peary caribou across the sea ice between the Arctic Islands. These High Arctic caribou are often forced to leave some areas because an ice cover forms on the ground, sealing off their food supply. The intense spring sun melts the snow cover, and meltwater percolates through to the still-frozen ground beneath and refreezes. The build-up of ice, sometimes reaching depths of three to four inches, covers the low-growing plants on which the caribou feed. With this sudden loss of their food supply, the animals are forced to make long treks across the sea ice to reach other islands where snow conditions are better and food is available. These caribou migrate to prevent starvation, not merely to calve. Though the crossings cover distances of fifty miles or more across shifting sea ice, the trails head compass-straight to small, low-lying islands in the vast arctic sea, even crossing wide open cracks in the ice. On the huge lakes of the barren-lands, caribou trails also run perfectly straight, even though the animals may be far out of sight of the shore.

I have observed one caribou migration that convinced me that learning or navigation was involved. In the spring of 1976 the Kaminuriak herd made a highly unusual migration. Normally these caribou winter in the forests of northern Manitoba and move northeast to their traditional calving area in spring. In 1975, however, they failed to make the southward migration in fall, moving north instead to winter on the tundra northwest of Baker Lake. The following spring they returned unerringly to their traditional calving area by travelling first east and then south, opposite to the usual pattern. Those animals clearly knew where they were and where they wanted to go.

The caribou are superbly adapted to survive and travel in the rigorous northern environment, and they have evolved to cope with the normal hazards of the spring migration. But under certain conditions, the migration may become a journey of hardship and danger for the females. By April poor nutrition, combined with the demands of the growing foetus, have usually reduced the cow's reserves of fat to less than half what she carried in the autumn. The arduous journey to the calving grounds expends further energy at a time when the growth of the foetus is also making its greatest demands on her. The energy drain on the cow becomes severe when deep soggy snow or frequent blizzards make travelling difficult. During the 1980 spring migration of the Porcupine herd, I saw cows so exhausted from fighting deep snow that they were sleeping soundly enough that I could walk up and touch them. They were bedded down among large groups of feeding animals and did not even hear their companions move away when I approached.

Difficult travelling conditions, following a hard winter during which the caribou have contended with deep snow or icy crusts, may in extreme cases so weaken the cows as to imperil the survival of the calves they carry. In 1962 the Kaminuriak caribou suffered the loss of almost all their calves. The previous winter's record-breaking snow depths, and the deep snow along the spring migration routes, apparently weakened the cows so much that fewer than five per cent of the calves they produced that June survived until autumn.

If spring comes quickly along the migration route, the caribou face another danger from northern rivers in break-up. At first open leads of flowing water occur along the river's edge, while the main body of ice remains intact in the centre of the river. At this stage the caribou must swim the frigid water at one shore, flounder out onto the solid ice, walk across the ice, plunge into the other open stretch, and swim to the opposite shore. Then when the river finally breaks up, huge chunks of ice grind and tumble together in the swollen current with an ominous roar. Ice jams form in bends and narrow places until the pressure of water dammed up behind them bursts through, carrying the obstruction downstream with explosive force. Huge blocks slide up on the shores, gouging furrows in the banks and smashing willows. Yet so strong is the drive of the cows to continue their trek that they often plunge recklessly into the ice-choked rivers, trying to thread their way through the chaos of tumbling pans. Many are crushed or drowned. Some clamber up on large pieces of ice only to be swept downstream and dumped into the mêlée again by the churning river. The migrating cows of the Porcupine herd often reach the Porcupine River at break-up, but press on heedless of the danger. The Thelon River presents a similar barrier to the Beverly herd.

The greatest hazard to the caribou during their journey to the calving grounds comes from the wolves. On the barren-lands the spring migration of the caribou is accompanied by a migration of wolves. During winter and spring, wolves in central Canada depend almost exclusively on caribou for food; there is no other prey available in significant numbers. Wolves kill snowshoe hares, ptarmigan, foxes, or other small animals when they can, but these species simply cannot provide adequate food for the wolves over the course of a winter. Perhaps no other carnivore depends more totally on one species of prey than does the wolf on the caribou of the central barrens during the winter. In other parts of the caribou's range — for example, in Alaska, the Yukon, and the mountainous parts of the Northwest Territories and British Columbia — moose and mountain sheep and other ungulates provide the wolves with alternate prey. Since these animals do not migrate to the same extent as do the caribou, they provide food for the wolves when the caribou are absent. Wolves on these ranges are usually territorial, with packs of related individuals defending an area that varies in size depending on the density of the wolf population and the availability of

prey. Only when the seasonal migrations of the caribou bring them into the wolves' territories do they too become part of the prey. When they leave again, the wolves generally do not follow, although there may be a few unattached wolves that do wander with the caribou. In Alaska's McKinley National Park, for instance, wolves sometimes prey heavily on caribou in the summer, but when the caribou leave in autumn the wolves switch their hunting to sheep and moose.

The wolves on the winter ranges of caribou in central Canada apparently do not defend specific territories. When the caribou gather in the early spring, wolf packs follow them; hundreds of wolves share the relatively small area occupied by the caribou. In the spring of 1979 I estimated that over 500 wolves occupied a 2000-square-mile area near the tree-line north of Yellowknife. That same winter, hunters killed over 1100 wolves from the caribou ranges near Coppermine. The density of wolves may reach levels as high as one wolf per two square miles, a ratio that is unknown among territorial wolves, even in areas where prey is very abundant. How these wolves avoid fighting when they meet, as do territorial wolves when one pack violates another's territory, is unknown. Because of the great difficulties of following tundra wolves over their remote and rugged ranges, almost nothing has been learned about their social organization. In fact, there is some question whether the groups of wolves seen on the central Canadian caribou ranges are packs in the traditional sense, or merely ever-changing associations of individuals.

When the caribou leave the forests and head onto the tundra, many of the wolves follow them, but others stay behind. Thus the wolves on the winter ranges include both timber wolves, those that remain to den in the forests, and tundra wolves, those that follow the caribou onto the barrens and there raise their young. Some veteran trappers insist that the tundra wolves move out onto the barrens ahead of the caribou and wait for them. Such movements may occur in years during which late thaws delay the caribou migration and wolves must go on ahead to dig dens before their pups are whelped in late May. My studies of the wolves associated with the Bathurst herd, however, indicated that they kept pace with the caribou, following the migration for some distance before stopping to den.

Many of the wolves that were marked with radio transmitter collars travelled 200 miles or more from the winter ranges before denning on the barrens, and some went all the way from the forests north of Yellowknife to the caribou calving grounds east of Bathurst Inlet, a distance of almost 400 miles. Other long-distance movements of wolves following caribou have been reported from the range of the Western Arctic herd in Alaska and also between the Thelon River and the winter ranges of the Beverly herd in northern Saskatchewan.

As the migration proceeds, pairs of wolves drop out to den when they find suitable sites, usually in sandy eskers, particularly where the roots of willows or birches bind the soil and keep it from collapsing. The dens are often located near sedgy ponds or potholes, where the wolves obtain drinking water and hunt for the nesting birds and small rodents that, in part, sustain them and their pups while the caribou are absent. Many of the den sites are traditional, occupied year after year.

When caribou are concentrated in large groups in late winter and spring, wolves find it easy to make kills. Many of the caribou, particularly calves, are weak at winter's end. On the other hand, the wolf pups born the previous year are almost full-grown and have gained sufficient experience to become successful members of a hunting group. Calves and adults in poor condition usually constitute a high proportion of the wolves' victims. The vulnerability of different age groups depends on the severity of the winter, with the young and old animals weakening most quickly under difficult conditions. But wolves are capable of catching healthy caribou if there are few weak or injured ones.

Packs hunt in several ways. Most often they "test" bands of caribou by chasing them and watching for animals that fall behind or veer from the group. These individuals are then pursued. The wolves try to gain an advantage by cutting corners on fleeing caribou when they turn, or by positioning themselves between a separated animal and the band it seeks to rejoin. Wolves also ambush caribou on trails between lakes. Other hunting strategies include driving caribou towards a hidden pack member, or chasing a large group into the deep soft snow at the lake edge where they pile up and flounder, giving the hunters time to close in.

Wolves attack caribou at the head and neck or shoulder, not by "hamstringing" the legs as is popularly believed. A full-grown wolf weighs eighty to a hundred pounds, more than a caribou calf in its first winter. Wolves usually grab calves by the neck or crush their skulls. With adult caribou they may slam into the animal, trying to knock it off its feet, grab a hindquarter, or slash at the shoulder to weaken it. They may also seize and hang onto the muzzle or trachea and suffocate the prey. Cows brought to bay may try to defend themselves with their antlers, but usually ineffectually; once the wolves have caught up with an animal, death comes quickly.

Wolves feed first on the tongue and throat of their kill and then tear open the flank to reach the rich internal organs. Wolves hunting actively in cold weather require at least five pounds of meat a day, and will eat much more if it is available. Thus an average-sized pack of five to ten animals will completely devour a small caribou in one or two days, then kill again. In my experience wolves on the range of the Bathurst herd almost always completely consume their kills in the spring and winter. Similar observations have been made in other parts of the Northwest Territories, the Yukon, and Alaska. All that remains when the wolves leave are the hooves and antlers, a few scraps of hide and scattered hair, and the stomach with its contents. Even the long bones of the legs are usually crushed and devoured. Ravens, jays, foxes, and wolverines scavenge at the kill while the wolves are away resting between meals.

It has been suggested that wolves kill extra caribou as the migration passes through the area where they intend to den, so that they will have carcasses to feed on after the caribou leave. I have not seen evidence of such behaviour in spring, although I have observed surplus killing of calves from the big caribou herds of mid-summer. Even without leftover carcasses wolves can survive and raise pups during the summer. The timber wolves that remain within the tree-line after the caribou leave subsist and raise their young on small mammals, birds, even insects and fish. The wolves that follow the cows and calves can usually find some caribou throughout the summer, since the mature bulls lag several weeks behind the cows and often scatter over the tundra where the wolves are denning, instead of going all the way to the calving grounds. Wolves are wide-ranging and resourceful hunters; even where caribou are scarce, they can find and kill them. Cows and calves return to the regions where the wolves den by mid- to late July, just as the pups are growing rapidly and need plenty of food that is high in energy and protein. Pups survive better and grow faster in areas where caribou are present during much of the summer than in areas where they are absent. Even if caribou are around, however, tundra wolves obtain part of their summer diet from ground squirrels, voles, lemmings, and breeding birds and their eggs.

But in the cold northern spring, before the land awakes to the abundance of summer, caribou and wolf are one. When the long lines of caribou set out on their yearly journey, the wolves follow. So it has been for ten thousand years. Together they travel onto the barren-lands to renew their kinds, hunter and hunted bound together in a relationship as ancient as their will to survive.

Pages 20-21: A band of spring migrants crosses overflow on the ice of the Whitestone River, Yukon.

Page 25: Caribou bands feeding at sunset, Schaeffer Mountain, Yukon.

Pages 26-27: Spring migration in the Keele Range, Yukon. The bulges under the hides of the animals in the foreground are caused by the larvae of warble flies, which will soon eat their way through the skin and drop to the ground to pupate.

Pages 28-29: Long lines of caribou move along open gravel bars on the Whitestone River, Yukon.

Page 29: Cows plunge into open water in the Porcupine River, Yukon, from intact ice in the middle of the river.

Page 30: Wolf near a kill on the McCrea River, Northwest Territories.

Pages 32-33: Migrating caribou rest during a snowstorm, Dubawnt River, Northwest Territories.

Page 35: Mazes of trails criss-cross the surface of the Surprise River system, Northwest Territories.

Page 36: Spring break-up on the barren-lands, Keewatin District, Northwest Territories.

Page 37: Caribou feed along the ridges of Schaeffer Mountain above the Old Crow River, Yukon. Old Crow Mountain looms in the background.

Pages 38-39: Small band moving at sunset, Schaeffer Mountain, Yukon.

Page 41 (upper): Migration trail, Surprise River, Northwest Territories.

Page 41 (lower): Caribou moving along one path in the maze of trails on the Surprise River, Northwest Territories.

Page 42 (upper): Cows move in single file along a trail cut in deep snow, near Old Crow, Yukon.

Page 42 (lower): A band of migrants descends the steep banks of the Porcupine River, Yukon, following the deeply cut trails of thousands that have preceded them.

Page 43 (left): A cow, exhausted from fighting deep snow along the migration trail, lies sleeping amid the feeding craters of her band, Schaeffer Mountain, Yukon.

Page 43 (right): A pair of oldsquaw ducks rests on candled ice, Bathurst herd calving grounds, Northwest Territories.

Page 44: Remains of a wolf kill, Chambeuil Lake, Saskatchewan.

Calving
A birthright of snow

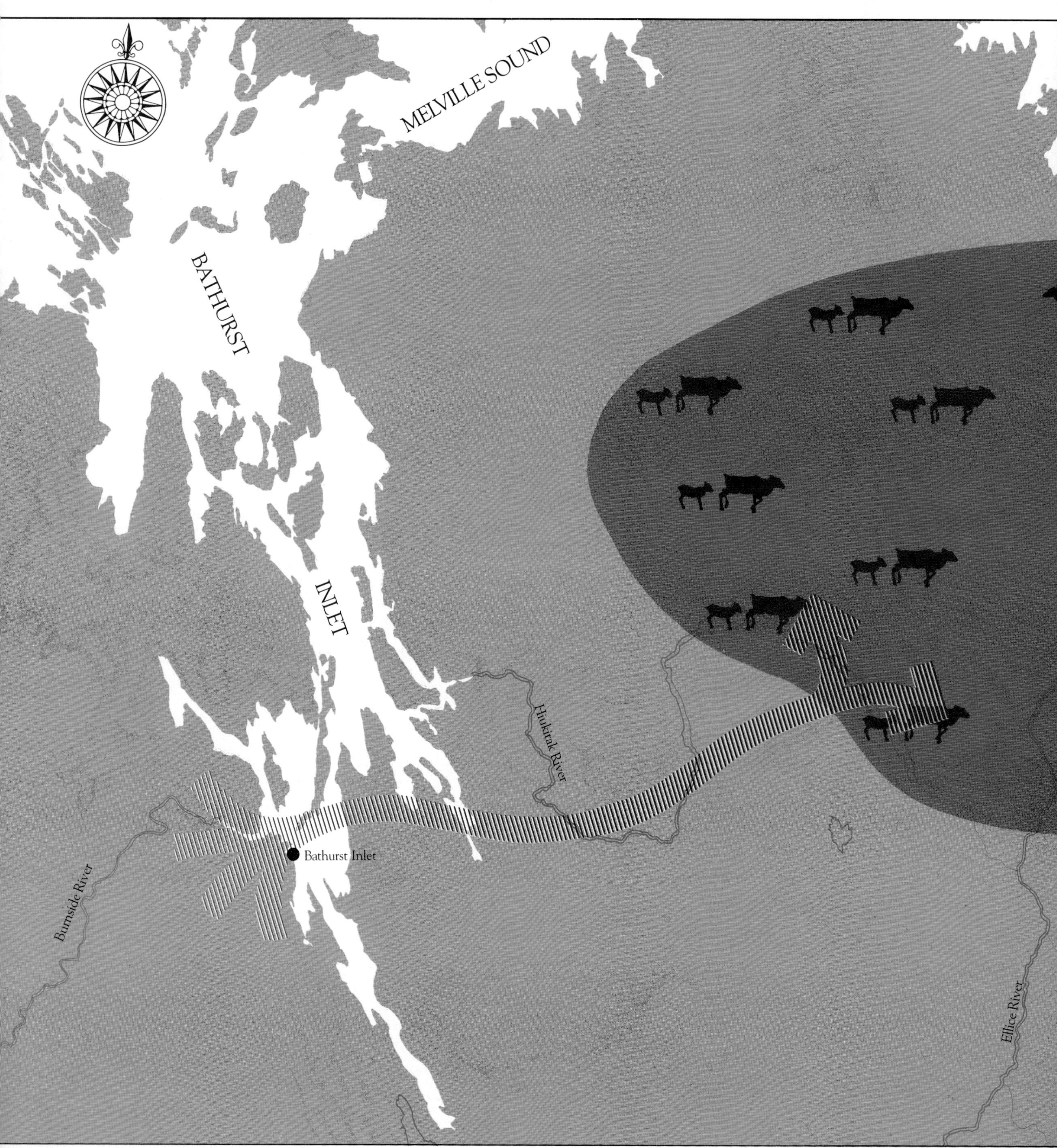

Calving grounds of the Bathurst herd

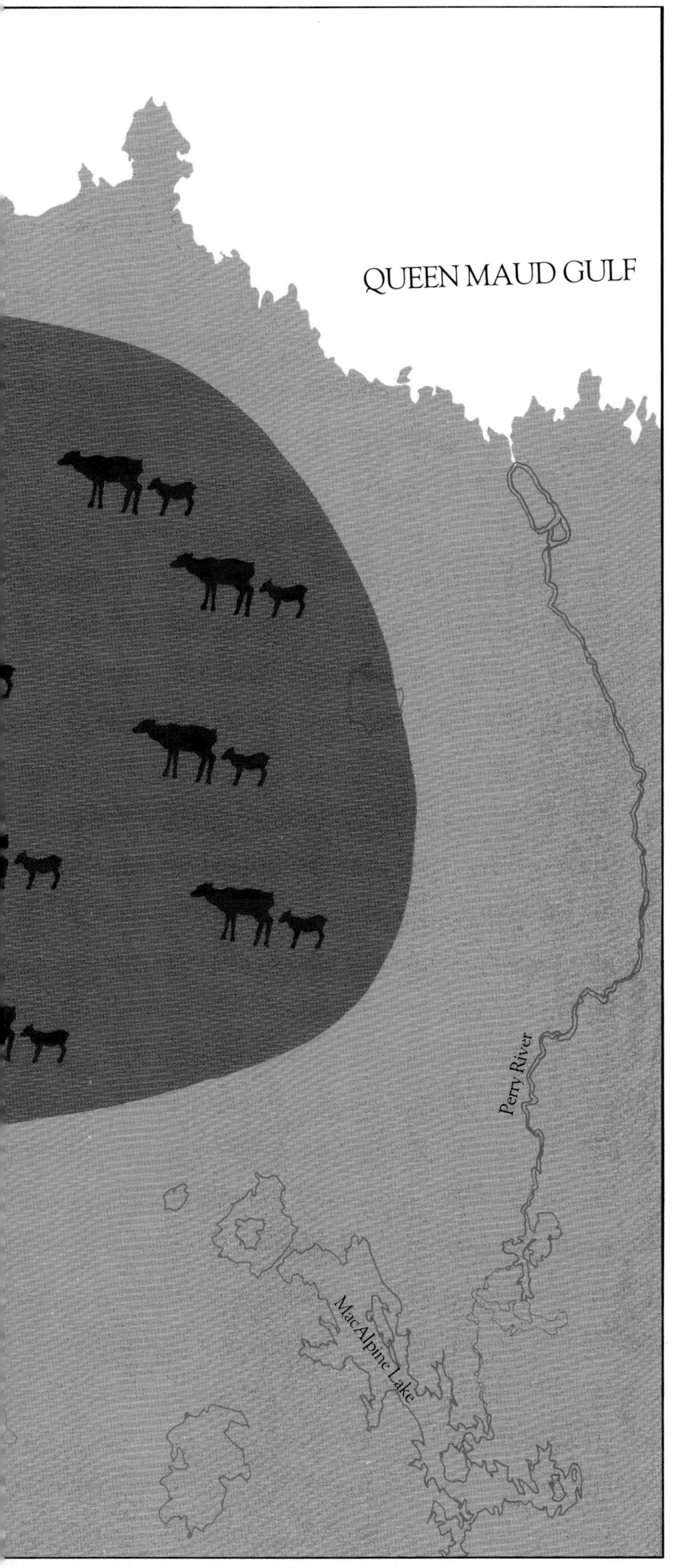

There are certain places on this earth that are special to animals. They will travel thousands of miles and endure incredible hardships to return to these, the places of their birth, there to pass on life to another generation. Thus the green turtle finds its way through leagues of trackless sea to one tiny island and lays its eggs in the sand of the very beach where it was born. A skein of geese cleaving the night skies of spring finally settles on the one marsh that contains its continuity with the past. The salmon battles its way up currents and waterfalls, nosing inexorably into smaller and smaller forks and tributaries until at last, ragged and exhausted, it fins out a nest in the same gravel from which it emerged. So it is with the caribou. The cows heavy with young return each spring to that one piece of tundra where they themselves began their endless journey.

The cow with one antler, plodding along in a file of over one hundred and fifty caribou, had nearly reached that goal. She walked head down, following the animal ahead of her by two body lengths, her hooves splashing in the puddles on the light blue ice of Bathurst Inlet. The group's lead animal stopped, sniffing at the hole in the ice around which her nose had detected the odour of a bearded seal. Behind her the line halted.

The cow with one antler lowered her head to drink briefly the slushy water from a puddle, then looked out over the ice. The sun burned brightly in the May sky, its glare exploding off the ice and snow and water. Through the shimmering waves of reflected heat three other long lines of migrating caribou were moving ahead of her band. The most distant animals swam and wavered in the mirage, first appearing as long-legged giants towering above the ice, then almost vanishing. Here and there the dark forms of seals lay near their breathing holes or along cracks in the ice. Every few seconds one lifted its head to glance around for its ancient enemy the polar bear and then collapsed again in lethargy.

The nearly year-old calf following the cow moved forward and tried to suckle. The cow turned away and put her head down to threaten him with her antler. He moved back. This calf was one of about fifteen that remained with the group; many others had already left their mothers and fallen behind, but this calf persisted faithfully. The lead animal, her curiosity satisfied, started to walk again and the line trailed after her.

Upon reaching the eastern shore of the inlet, the caribou immediately fanned out and began feeding. They grazed up a southwest-facing slope, gradually working their way to the top. There several other bands of migrants lay resting and chewing their cuds. The new arrivals spread out and found room among the boulders that the retreating glaciers had dropped everywhere across this land. The cow with one antler bent her front legs and eased to the ground, while her yearling calf lay down a few feet away. The cow began to chew her cud as she gazed out over the rocky hills that cradled the inlet. On nearby hills still more groups lay resting or grazing, silhouetted against the sky. The land was alive with caribou, each pregnant female filled with the same urge to reach the place of calving.

During the evening the sun slid along the northern horizon, gilding the undersides of clouds that hung along the Arctic coast. Sounds like the tinkling of chimes floated on the wind as Lapland longspurs flew into the golden air and fell fluttering back to earth singing, each male claiming his territory on the drab tundra. When the sun dipped below the horizon, the air grew cold and gradually the birds stopped displaying. Only a white fox yapping in the distance and the faint cries of gulls broke the silence.

In the early morning the cow with one antler rose and fed again, then began walking eastward. Others fell in behind her. As they lined out into the glare of the rising sun, long marching columns were still coming out of the southwest across the vast blue and white of the inlet.

The cow led her group over the rugged hills for three hours before stopping to feed and rest again. She kept an east-northeasterly course and took the terrain as it came, rather than contouring or following the drainages. When they moved off again in the early afternoon, a different cow left first and thus became the leader. The migrants fed and rested and travelled once more before the sun set; then they stopped during the few hours of twilight, which were all that remained of night at these high latitudes in May.

That evening low clouds rolled in from the coast. Throughout the next day the sun shone like a pale yellow orb in the mist, as the line of caribou climbed each hill in its turn and disappeared into the fog shrouding the summits. The pattern of travel, feed, and rest remained much the same as on the previous day; by sunset they had covered the thirty miles from Bathurst Inlet to the Hiukitak River.

The sounds of life returning to the river reached the ears of the caribou as they neared the edge of the valley. The river had not yet completely broken up. In some places dirty brown water flowed over intact stretches of ice. In other sections, chunks and pans of blue and white ice floated in a giant patchwork against the dark water. An incessant chorus of oldsquaws floated up from the eddies, as the ducks splashed, dived, and chased each other in the excitement of courtship. From somewhere in the dusk a flock of geese called raucously for a moment, then fell silent. Cottongrass covered long slopes leading down to the river, in contrast to the rocky hills through which the group had been passing. In the fading light, feeding caribou were barely visible, their pale coats blending with the dead grass and patches of snow. One by one the arriving animals descended into the gathering gloom to join the others.

The Hiukitak valley acted as both an oasis and a highway for living things travelling through the land. For the next two days as the caribou trailed along the river, other moving and crying creatures continually enlivened the drabness of the spring tundra. Flock after flock of geese flew up the river calling loudly, sometimes the dark Vees of Canadas or whitefronts, sometimes mixed flocks of snow and blue geese that presented a startling hallucination. When a flock passed in front of a snowy slope or stretch of ice, the white birds seemed to disappear and the blues stood out sharply. But the next instant the white snows flashed against dark water or bare ground, and the blues vanished. Lines of whistling swans passed silently like ghosts in the mist. Hurrying knots of plovers and sandpipers turned and twisted simultaneously in flight, obeying a single impulse, as they followed the bends of the river. Like the caribou, these birds were returning "home," navigating by senses that can only be guessed at.

In bare patches, voles and lemmings scurried along pathways and tunnels through the sedges. These small rodents had passed the winter beneath the insulating blanket of snow, enjoying temperatures at ground level many degrees warmer and more stable than the frigid air above. Although they had been active all winter beneath this cover, they were seeing daylight for the first time in seven months.

Above the slopes a rough-legged hawk hung on rapidly beating wings, keen dark eyes searching the tundra below. Suddenly he folded his wings and dropped. A moment later he flapped aloft, clutching in his talons a red-backed vole. He carried his prize to a perch on a nearby outcrop and began tearing it apart. During the past week scores of hunting rough-legs had passed high over the river, as had floppy-winged snowy owls that coursed low over the tundra like huge white moths. The abundance of these predatory birds indicated that the lemmings and voles

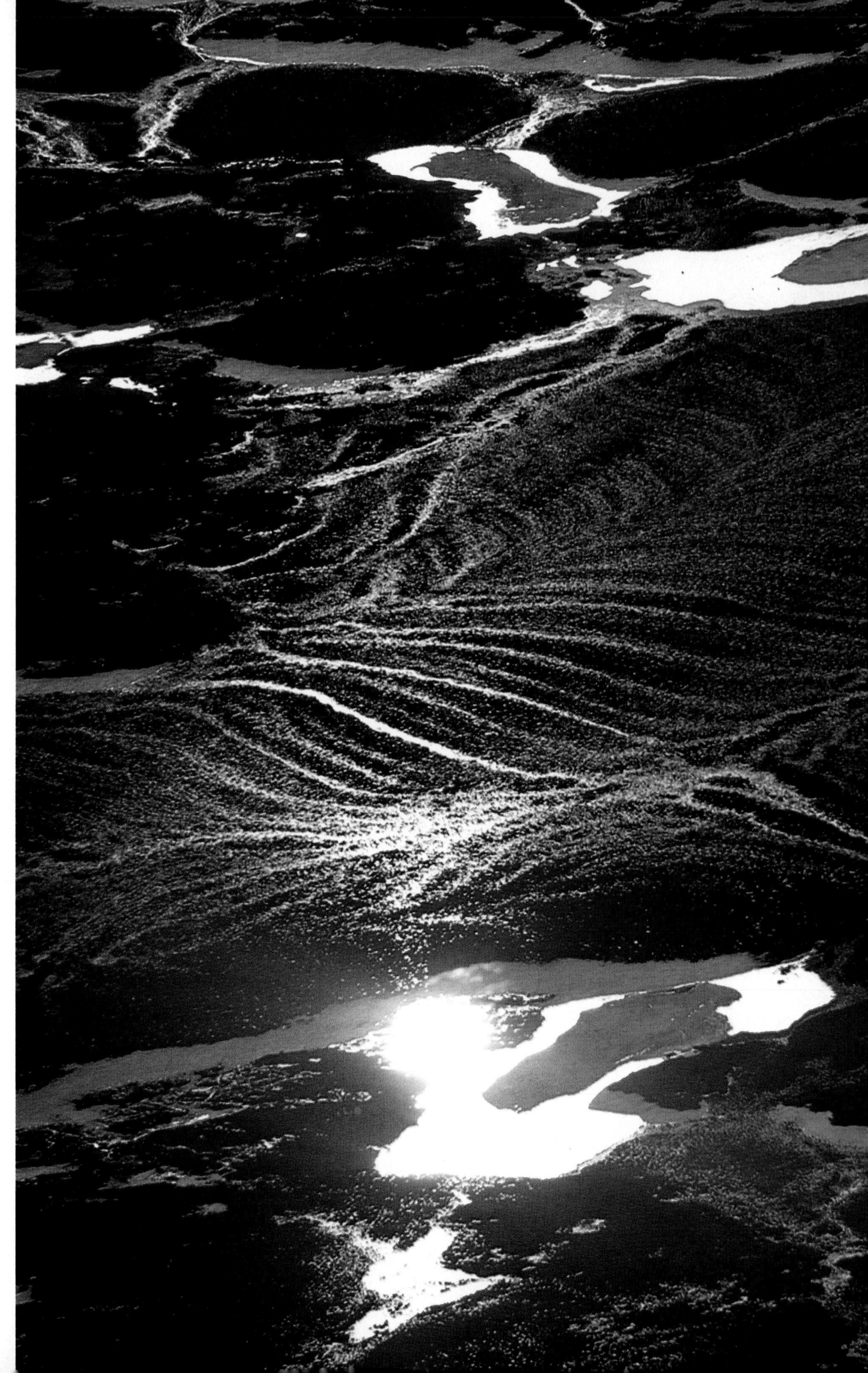

were reaching the peak of their three- to four-year population cycles. This year there would be many raptor nests with many downy young.

The caribou kept mostly to the higher ground, twice passing above herds of musk-oxen feeding in the valley. From a distance the dark and massive beasts grazed with antediluvian slowness, as though the very stones of earth had come to life and moved over the tundra. Several small musk-ox calves, already two or three weeks old, trailed behind their shaggy mothers.

The caribou followed the Hiukitak as long as it flowed from the east, but when the river curved away northward they again struck northeast. Here the land changed. The hills gave way to a vast plain of small lakes, separated by ridges standing only a few dozen feet above the lakes and broken everywhere by outcrops, shattered rocks, and glacial boulders. Yellow and black splotches of crustose lichens painted these bare bones of the land. Small meadows and swales of cottongrass lay among the ridges.

The low cloud had burned away, and under the bright sun the winter's snow was quickly melting. Dark rocks and tufts of vegetation poking through the snow absorbed heat and hurried the transformation from winter to spring. Meltwater percolated down through the sodden snow, to flow along the frozen soil and over the ice in streams until it puddled up on the lakes. Spiders and small insects, roused from their winter dormancy, crawled about in the sun.

When the caribou reached this country of broken ridges, they slowed. They were getting close to the goal that had drawn them across the many miles. Now they travelled only once or twice a day, usually in mid-morning or late afternoon, stopping often to feed and chew their cuds. The band was breaking up. Twenty-five animals headed north up a long narrow lake that the rest crossed. That afternoon more cows stayed behind as the rest of the group moved off.

By the fifth of June the cow with one antler remained in the company of seventeen other pregnant females in a small meadow of cottongrass tussocks on a boulder-strewn ridge. The urge to travel had almost left her; she had moved only a couple of miles during the past two days. The country was familiar; she had been born only a few miles from here. Every spring she had returned, first at her mother's heels and later, guided by her own instincts, to bear her young.

As the time of birth approached, the cow with one antler grew more intolerant of the yearling calf that had stayed by her side throughout the past year. Now, whenever he approached closely, she drove him away, lowering her head to threaten him with her antler or rearing to strike with her front hooves. Sometimes she chased him for several yards. Under this constant rebuff the yearling finally gave up trying to stay with her. One afternoon he wandered off with a small group of fellow yearlings that had been similarly rejected.

Next morning, as the caribou fed slowly along the ridge, the cow with one antler suddenly stopped. She lowered her head and opened her mouth as her sides heaved with the force of the contractions inside. The other animals fed on. She began to follow, but soon another contraction seized her and she lay down in a small, snowless patch of cottongrass. She rested for a while on her chest, her tail lifting and falling occasionally. Then, as the pale amber birth sac began to bulge from her body, she rolled over flat on her side.

Her labour lasted about an hour. Most of the time she lay quietly with her tail lifting rhythmically and her sides heaving. Sometimes, as the contractions grew violent, she threw back her head, arching her back and kicking out her hind legs. Repeatedly she stood up and turned around several times, as though trying to make herself comfortable before lying down again. At last, as the cow stood up once more, the calf slid out and plopped onto the tundra.

The birth sac broke as it hit the ground, and the glistening calf immediately began struggling to free itself. The cow, her hindquarters stained with the bright blood of birth, turned to sniff and lick her newborn. She worked vigorously, her rough tongue serving to both clean and dry the calf's fur and to stimulate its circulation. While she attended the calf, her contractions continued; within minutes the placenta dropped to the ground. The cow then turned from the calf to eat the bloody afterbirth, shaking her head to bite the slippery, floppy mass.

As the cow chewed the afterbirth, the tiny male calf struggled to his feet. He stood shakily for a few seconds, his back arched and rear legs bent awkwardly, with the centre part of the leg almost parallel to the ground. Then he tottered to the cow's side and put his small head under her body. Somehow the infant knew that nourishment was to be found beneath the cow, but did not know instinctively where to find the udder. The calf nuzzled the cow's fur between her front legs, then rooted along her belly. As he searched, the mother turned her head and licked his hindquarters. At last the calf found the swollen udder and began to nurse. The little animal suckled

strongly for about half a minute and then collapsed, exhausted by the effort. The cow lay down, sheltering the tiny form with her body against the strengthening north-east wind. She began to lick the calf again, first the entire length of the body and then concentrating on the face and rear end.

Throughout the morning the cow lay beside her newborn, licking and smelling him. Occasionally she walked a few feet away to graze on the yellow and grey flowers of the cottongrass. Then in the early afternoon she arose and moved off several yards. She turned towards the calf and lowered her head, bobbing it up and down a couple of times and grunting. At this call the calf got up and tottered towards her, falling once on the uneven tussocks. The cow allowed her offspring to nurse for several seconds, then walked away again and repeated the call. The calf crept after her unsteadily, his legs spread wide for balance. The hunched posture, arched back, and lowered neck proclaimed the young one's recent advent into the world, although his reddish-brown fur was now dry and fluffy. Pacing herself to the calf's progress, calling and bobbing her head for encouragement when he faltered, the cow led her newborn in his first steps in a life of never-ending travel.

The two walked half a mile before halting in the lee of some large boulders. The cow lay down and began to lick the calf again. During the afternoon and early evening the wind increased steadily. The cow and calf remained behind the boulders, getting up occasionally to allow the calf to nurse. By midnight the wind had risen to a whistling gale. Soft wet snow driven parallel to the ground began to plaster the rocks with a greyish pallor.

The blizzard blasted all sign of life from the land. Three pairs of snow geese, nesting on an outcrop across the ridge from the caribou, flattened themselves against their nests as the sodden snow drifted around them. Longspurs and ptarmigan, usually so prominent with their aerial displaying and calling, cowered behind rocks and in depressions among the tussocks. The ground squirrels simply returned to their burrows and curled up on nests of dry grass.

Wind and snow battered the land for the rest of the night and for two more days and nights. The snow geese abandoned their nests. Longspurs and horned larks hopped and scratched about, looking for seeds in the few patches of ground and finding little. Without fuel for their high metabolism, they chilled and died by the thousands. The cow and her calf stayed sheltered behind their boulders for most of the time. Occasionally the cow moved to feed in a nearby swale, but soon returned to the

calf. Once the youngster ventured out with her but was blown off his feet as he tried to nurse; thereafter he stayed under shelter. During the storm a few other groups of caribou passed nearby, drifting before the wind like ghosts, barely visible through the driving snow.

When at last the wind began to subside, caribou started to appear among the rocks of the ridge. More had sheltered there than had been apparent earlier. Some of the cows were followed by calves still unsteady on their feet; they had obviously come into the world during the storm. Although the blizzard had killed many calves, it seemed incredible that any of these small spindly-legged creatures could have survived such an onslaught. But they were of hardy stock, selected by millennia of hardship on the barren-lands — their birthright snow and storm.

The caribou's first need was to feed heavily, then rest and ruminate. The cow with one antler joined approximately twenty other females whose calves had all been born within the past four days. While she fed, her calf made his own first tentative attempts at grazing, plucking haphazardly at the cottongrass. But he still nursed eagerly. Usually he stood beside the cow as he suckled, while she licked his anus and hindquarters, but sometimes he ran up behind her and stuck his head between her legs. As he fed, he bunted the udder with his head to let down the milk. At one point another calf approached the cow as she grazed. She lowered her head to its level, with her forelegs straight and her head pointing slightly inward so that her antler was directed at the stranger. When the calf failed to heed this ritual threat, she hooked at it with her antler. The calf dodged to avoid the blow and returned to its mother.

For the rest of the day the caribou stayed together, moving slowly down the ridge, alternately feeding and resting. In the evening they joined another group of cows and calves, remaining with them during the twilight. All moved off together next morning.

The new snow melted quickly in the warmer weather that followed the blizzard. Rivers and streams now ran freely, and the ice on most lakes had "candled," forming vertical crystals that allowed the meltwater to percolate through to the lake below. Lakes that had been covered with soggy drifts and innumerable pools of meltwater when the caribou arrived, now offered an ideal surface for travelling. The only difficulties occurred at the lake edges where belly-deep drifts of snow remained. The caribou searched for easy ways on and off the lakes as they traversed the country.

In the afternoon, as the group was fording a stream, one of the calves was swept away. The current, which had already claimed the lives of several calves earlier that day, carried the bleating animal quickly downstream. The mother hurried along the bank after it, calling in reply, but when the calf managed to reach the shore a ledge of ice prevented it from clambering out. The calf clung there with its forelegs up on the ice. The cow walked to the edge of the ice grunting and bobbing her head as close as possible in front of her trapped young one. Thus encouraged, the calf gripped the ice with its small hooves and lurched out. On shore it shook mightily, sending silver droplets glittering in the sunlight. The mother licked its face and then led it at a swift trot back along the stream to the trails of the disappearing band.

As the group continued on, they merged with the cows and calves they met. By week's end the herd contained over a thousand cows, mostly accompanied by calves. Many yearlings had also joined the band, but for the most part they stayed together at the edge of the herd. The cow with one antler was now indistinguishable from the other cows, for all had shed their antlers soon after the birth of their calves. The urge to travel was reasserting itself. She walked steadily along in the growing herd, glancing back occasionally at the calf trotting close at her heels.

The calving grounds constitute the focal point of the immense travels of each herd of barren-ground caribou. To this traditional place of birth the females return year after year, though it encompasses as little as one or two per cent of the total area over which they range throughout their annual cycle. Indeed, we recognize and define each herd by the calving grounds it uses. Thus all the caribou that habitually travel to one distinct place to calve belong to one herd, although they may scatter widely during the rest of the year.

When the caribou arrive at the calving grounds after a migration that may span hundreds of difficult miles, they sense that they are "home." Cows that have been hurrying through the snow, covering fifteen or twenty miles a day, suddenly slow down. The long purposeful lines of migration break up into smaller and smaller wandering bands that move at a leisurely pace, grazing and resting. If travelling conditions are good, caribou may arrive at the calving area as much as a month before they give birth. Rather than passing blindly on, the growing number of pregnant females remain in the area, moving in large circular patterns until their time arrives.

Conversely, if storms or a late melt prevent the cows from reaching the calving grounds before the time of birth, they drop their calves en route. Such occurrences led some early biologists to assume that there were no fixed calving grounds, that caribou simply gave birth wherever they happened to be at the end of the gestation period. But this is not true. The females appear to know where they are going. If they are forced to give birth short of the true calving grounds, they do not stop for long; rather, they rejoin the migration as soon as the calves can travel. In fact, calves may die as the onrushing cows lead them across slush-covered lakes and ford frigid streams with shelves of ice along the shore. Some females even abandon their calves, so great is their drive to continue moving. It is clear from this behaviour that once the urge to migrate seizes them, the animals continue travelling until they recognize that they have reached the traditional calving grounds.

In the largest herds tens of thousands of cows may occupy the calving grounds; yet few large groups can be seen. Before giving birth the expectant cows disperse themselves relatively evenly over the landscape — one of the few times of the year when these gregarious creatures do so. Consequently, few groups number over fifty individuals, and the most common bands contain fewer than ten cows. The density of cows averages ten to twenty per square mile, rarely more than thirty per square mile; no concentrations exist to attract predators.

The segregation between the sexes, which began on the winter ranges, is virtually complete before the females reach the place of birth. Fewer than one or two per cent of the caribou on the calving grounds are males over one year of age; these are primarily immature animals — two- and three-year-olds. Most young bulls and many yearlings drop behind the cows during the latter stages of migration and arrive days afterwards. As a result, these young animals tend to gather on the edges of the area occupied by the pregnant cows, particularly in the direction from which the migration initially arrived.

After reaching the calving grounds, the cows seem content to rest frequently, lying on meadows of cottongrass tussocks or among the jumbled rocks on a ridge, recovering from the exertions of the migration. Their pale, winter-bleached coats blend perfectly with the straw-coloured cottongrass. Snow cover lies in patches on the ridge tops, and the small bands of caribou lying quietly there appear as simply a few more snowdrifts. Thus, inconspicuously, a part of the sombre arctic landscape, the caribou await the time of birth.

When the new generation finally arrives, it comes with a rush. Births occur remarkably synchronously in a caribou herd. Seventy-five per cent of the calves appear in a span of only five days, and two weeks encompass virtually all the births. At the peak of calving in a large herd, thousands of calves enter the world each day.

The calving period varies among herds and from year to year. Among the five major herds of the Canadian barrens, most calves are dropped during the first two weeks in June. In the Porcupine herd and the Arctic herds of northern Alaska and the Yukon, the first young appear in very late May and the first week of June. In interior Alaska calving starts two weeks earlier, before mid-May. Dates vary by as much as a week, however, and calves may also appear sooner on some parts of the calving grounds than on others. The calves on the northern half of the Kaminuriak calving grounds are often born a week earlier than on the southern half. Year-to-year changes in calving dates may be explained either by yearly differences in the date of the rut or by variations in the normal 228-day gestation period. Caribou apparently calve later following years with severe winters, probably because poor winter nutrition alters the gestation period.

It might be supposed that because so many calves come into the world at the same time, many births would be visible in the open vistas of the calving grounds. Actually, the birth of a caribou calf is difficult to witness. Cows become extremely wary just before they give birth. Moreover, the birth itself is accomplished remarkably quickly. The female lies down on a snowless patch of vegetation and goes into labour, the only sign of which may be the lifting of her tail and an occasional heaving of her sides. Within minutes, generally less than an hour, the birth sac emerges with the dark wet calf struggling inside. It takes a keen-eyed observer to pick out a cow in labour among a group lying amid jumbled boulders on a ridge.

The precise details of giving birth vary somewhat among individual animals. Calves may be born while the female lies on her side, but many cows stand up at the last moment to help the calf drop. Sometimes the birth membranes and placenta pop out with the calf enclosed in the birth sac; in other cases more labour ensues and the membranes and placenta are not passed for several hours. The cow may stand to tend the calf or graze with the birth membranes only partially passed. In certain cases abnormally long retention of placental membranes causes the death of the cow. Placental retention usually occurs in herds infected with the disease brucellosis, sometimes called contagious abortion, whose existence in the Western Arctic herd of

Alaska and the Porcupine herd is well documented.

The average size of the calves is related to the size of the adults in the herd. Female barren-ground caribou in the Northwest Territories, the Yukon, and northern Alaska weigh about 200 pounds, and produce calves averaging eleven to thirteen pounds in weight. By contrast, female woodland caribou and the big caribou of interior Alaska weigh 300 pounds or more, and their calves are proportionately larger. Individual weights, however, vary considerably. Live calves weighing as little as eight and a half pounds have been recorded. Most of the differences in weight among the various herds may be attributed to differences in the abundance and quality of food. Thus in the Arctic, where the growing season is the shortest and the growth rate and standing crop of plants the lowest, the caribou are the smallest. In interior Alaska the longer growing season and greater abundance of forage are reflected in the larger size of the caribou.

Barren-ground caribou produce only one calf each spring; twinning is virtually non-existent. Moreover, in all herds eighty to ninety-five per cent of the adult females are pregnant each year, except following extremely hard winters. The only variation that has been observed between herds is the age of first reproduction. In herds grazing on good ranges, a few two-year-olds and many three-year-olds give birth, while in other herds few cows reach maturity before the fourth year. Because both the pregnancy rate and the number of young change little from year to year, the reproductive potential of caribou is essentially fixed. In contrast, other species of deer in North America can take immediate advantage of favourable conditions to increase their populations. With productive ranges and good weather, white-tailed and mule deer, moose, and wapiti can produce twins and even triplets. Their fawns and calves may breed and give birth at the age of one year. Conversely, when conditions are poor many females of these species become barren and maturation is delayed.

Immediately after giving birth, the female caribou begins to lick, smell, and nuzzle the newborn calf. When the placenta is passed, she consumes it. The cow alternates between licking the calf and eating the afterbirth, from which she obtains hormones that stimulate the flow of milk. Within the first two hours and sometimes within minutes of birth, the calf stands and suckles, drinking in life-giving warmth and nourishment. Caribou milk, containing about twenty per cent fat, is the richest known milk next to that of marine mammals. During the first few hours the female alternately lies beside the calf licking it and grazes nearby. Finally she moves off a few yards and calls with a gutteral grunt. She may also lower her head and bob it at the calf. Her call and head bob encourage the calf to follow. It immediately wobbles to its feet and totters after her.

A calf at birth does not instinctively recognize its mother, nor does it fear other creatures, including humans. The newborn calf will follow anything. If a person chases away the cow and approaches a calf, the little animal readily accepts the intruder. It allows itself to be patted and eagerly sucks on offered fingers. If the person walks away, the young one will totter behind, bleating loudly when it cannot keep up. The calf identifies the first living thing it sees as a parent, and after a few days accepts it as the proper object for socialization throughout the rest of its life. If newborn calves are captured and hand-reared, they never develop fear of man, even if returned to the wild.

Thus each calf must learn to know and recognize its own mother. Through constant contact during the first few days of life, the female and her young familiarize themselves with each other's characteristics and establish a close bond. The mother first learns to recognize her young by its distinctive smell as she sniffs, licks, and nuzzles it. Later the cow and calf become familiar with each other's voice, the female calling to summon the calf when she moves and the young one bleating with distress if separated from its mother. This vocal communication allows the cow to call her calf if she senses danger, and enables the pair to keep track of each other in the confusion of a large moving herd. Finally, the mother and young may learn to distinguish each other by sight. Each of these forms of recognition improves with time. Soon they will be able to identify each other even in the huge herds that form later in the summer.

During the critical first days of life, while the cow is forming the bond with her calf, she will threaten any other calf that approaches. If it persists, she will kick at it or chase it away with lowered antlers. The cow also drives off her own yearling just before she gives birth. She must dissociate herself from the previous year's offspring to devote all her attention to the new one. The rejected yearlings, finding themselves suddenly alone, usually seek each other's company and travel together throughout the summer. Some yearlings, however, remain as near their mothers as the cows will allow, and try to associate with them and the new calves. In some herds, trios consisting of cow, calf, and yearling are frequently seen, suggesting that yearlings may successfully rejoin their mothers after the cows' period of intolerance is past.

These acts of aggression by the cow towards other herd members ensure that nothing interferes with the development of the vital bond that will tie the calf to her throughout its first year.

As the calf is forming its attachment to the mother, it also rapidly gains strength and agility. During the first day the calf remains unsteady on its feet, with a hunched and awkward posture. Even so, it can stumble along behind its mother for long distances if she is disturbed and moves off. By the second day the seemingly clumsy youngster can outdistance a man on the treacherous footing of the tussock tundra. Within a few days the bond between cow and calf is firm; the mothers lead their offspring into the company of others. Now the lively calves can easily keep up with the travelling bands as they come together into ever-growing herds. Like the playful young of so many species, they frolic and jump, tearing in wide circles for several minutes before returning to their placidly grazing mothers.

The frisky youngsters often become mixed up with other calves or get left behind when the herd moves on. In the wake of a large group's passage, lost calves wander the tundra bleating for their mothers; cows backtrack searching for their missing young. Sometimes a lone female that has obviously lost her calf, as evidenced by her still-swollen udder, will follow other caribou with calves. The searching cow tries to approach the calves, and may even force her way between a calf and its mother. Such behaviour has led some observers to wonder whether these bereft females will adopt strange calves that have lost their mothers.

Adoption is most unlikely. When a searching cow approaches a lone calf, she sniffs it to ascertain if it is her own. Positive identification appears to require smell. If the calf is a stranger, the cow jumps back. She may even strike at it with her hooves or antlers if it tries to follow her as she trots away. Fortunately, females that have lost their calves are not easily deterred; they search long and diligently and often find them. They are commonly seen hurrying along the trail of a herd, leading a wayward calf back to the group. But for those calves that are never found, life is short. The guidance of an adult is vital for

coping with predators and the many other dangers of the northern environment.

Although calves initially depend completely on their mothers' milk, they begin to graze within days of birth. Even calves still wobbly on their feet may try to pluck a mouthful of sedge. The bacterial flora of the rumen develop within two weeks of birth, and thereafter the young animals become more and more independent for their nourishment. On their diet of rich milk and the nutritious first growth of plants, the calves grow rapidly, doubling in weight within the first two to three weeks. By mid-July suckling occurs infrequently, although occasional instances of nursing will be seen throughout the first year, and the calves are weaned onto the plants that will sustain them for the rest of their lives.

The tremendous drive that caribou feel to reach their traditional places of birth year after year suggests that these areas must have special attributes particularly suitable for the survival of the calves. Yet to the human eye the calving grounds seem bleak and inhospitable. Meltwater lies in pools on the frozen ground, the land is often shrouded in fog, and the wind whistles unceasingly among the stunted plants and bare rocks. Why do the caribou travel hundreds of miles to reach these stark places?

One answer lies in the relative scarcity of predators. The wolves that follow the caribou during much of the spring migration stop to dig dens before their pups are born in May; the caribou continue travelling until June. Thus most of the wolves are left behind. Even if wolves could follow the caribou to the calving grounds, conditions there are not suitable for denning. Wolves seek out well-drained sites such as sandy eskers or along the banks of major rivers where they can easily dig their complex tunnels. The calving grounds on the rocky uplands of Canada's barren-lands, or the soggy cottongrass plains of Alaska, with ground ice just below the surface, do not provide a suitable environment for denning. Moreover, resident wolf populations cannot develop on the calving grounds because none of their major prey live there year-round. With the exception of a few musk-oxen in the Canadian Arctic and moose along the occasional sheltered valley on the coastal plain of Alaska and the Yukon, there is nothing for wolves to eat except for that one vital month each spring when the caribou appear. In Newfoundland, where wolves were exterminated decades ago, several of the caribou herds no longer make spring migrations; they calve in the same areas where they spend the winter.

By travelling north to calve, or to higher elevations as do the herds of interior Alaska, the caribou also postpone the onslaught of the mosquitoes, blackflies, and warble flies that will torture them unmercifully later in the summer. Blood-sucking insects emerge as much as a month later on the calving grounds than on the ranges where the caribou winter. By migrating, the caribou ensure that the vital processes of birth, suckling, and bonding between the mother and infant take place undisturbed by the torment of insects. The size and strength of the calf increase dramatically during the first weeks of life; soon it can withstand the terrible drains of insect harassment better than at birth. For the cow, too, the demand on energy reserves as a result of nursing is greatest during these first few weeks before the calf can graze independently. An added energy loss caused by insect parasitism would be debilitating at this time.

A further factor in the choice of calving grounds may be protection from storms. Cold windy weather causes the death of numerous young calves. Wet snow or freezing rain accompanying the windchill increases the death rate, for rain destroys the insulative value of the caribou's fur and accelerates heat loss through evaporation. Observers on the calving grounds have reported instances of violent winds blowing nursing calves off their feet, and injuring animals crossing slippery, newly frozen ice. The broken ridges and boulders of the calving grounds, however, offer shelter from winds, and the higher elevations make it more likely that precipitation will fall as snow rather than as rain. Such shelter may provide the margin of survival in the cruel climate of the barren-lands.

Severe weather with a consequent loss of newborn calves from windchill is rare on the calving grounds of Alaska and the Yukon. Here an additional factor seems more important in the choice of calving areas: the early melting of snow cover, followed by the growth and budding of cottongrass. These sedge flowers supply concentrated nutrients at just the time when the energy demands on the female for nursing are greatest. Even in the rocky calving areas of the Canadian barrens, the ridges most heavily used by calving females are near cottongrass meadows.

Thus both spring migration and the choice of birthplace are adaptations to the northern environment. Similarly, the birth process itself and the behaviour of the cow during calving have evolved to ensure the survival of the barren-ground caribou in an open habitat where they are constantly threatened by predators.

Calving time is the only period during the year when caribou cannot feel secure in their usual defence against predators — running away. A cow in advanced labour or a newborn calf lies helpless before an enemy. Anything that contributes to avoiding predators and to shortening the vulnerable birth period is advantageous. The attachment of the placenta in caribou, for instance, is simpler than in many other ungulates. This adaptation, along with the fact that caribou produce only one young, means that the birth is accomplished easily, without long labour,

and the foetal membranes are not retained. Similarly, the rapid physical growth of the young, fuelled by the rich milk and the early development of grazing, gives the calf mobility in a world where moving means survival. Quick births and rapid development of the young also characterize the herding species of the African savannah like the wildebeest and zebra, which share with the caribou the problem of living in the open, easily visible to predators.

The wariness of the cows reaches its peak of the year just after their calves are born. Calving is the only period when cows will run from something without waiting to confirm the danger by scenting the intruder. The same animals that in winter, out of sheer curiosity, may trot towards a man or a wolf or even tolerate their approach to within a hundred yards will become alert to a figure appearing on the skyline and flee when it is a quarter of a mile or more away. Pregnant cows or those with new calves also flee at the mere sight of another caribou moving off or even assuming an alarm posture.

When a predator approaches a cow with a newborn calf, she tries to lead the calf away. She runs off a few feet and grunts to call the young one, then heads away once it begins to follow. The cow looks back regularly to check on the calf's progress and to encourage it with calls and bobs of the head. If the predator gets too close, the cow begins to dash in wide circles in an attempt to distract it, returning to the calf occasionally to offer encouragement. The calf keeps up as well as it can, but if it tires or if the mother outdistances it, the calf may lie down and remain motionless. Such a calf, well hidden among the cottongrass tussocks or low willows and dwarf birches common on the calving grounds, is all but invisible from even a few feet away. Moreover, the cow shows a remarkable ability to remember where her calf dropped from sight. After leading the predator away, the mother returns and calls to locate her young. Thus, although flight is the caribou's normal response to predators, hiding is also important during the first few days, as is the case with other deer.

The synchrony of births, which promotes the formation of groups of calves of a similar age, may also constitute an adaptation to the threat of predation. Calves of approximately the same age will appear alike to predators, a fact which may make it difficult for them to single out and chase down an individual animal. The larger the herd, the greater this potential for confusing a pursuer.

Despite these several adaptations, predators remain the greatest danger to newborn caribou. The calf's small size, scarcely larger than an arctic hare, makes it vulnerable to many carnivores — not just the largest ones like wolves and bears, but also wolverines, foxes, lynx, and golden eagles. Even though these hunters may be scarcer on the calving grounds than on other portions of the range, they nevertheless kill many calves.

The wolves that do travel to the calving grounds respond instinctively when they find a concentration of helpless calves, killing far in excess of their needs. Only the choicest parts of these calves are consumed: the brain, tongue, and milk curds in the stomach. Wolves in some numbers visit most of the calving grounds in Canada and Alaska, and several instances of such surplus killing have been reported. Indeed, wolves are such efficient hunters of caribou calves that the small groups of woodland caribou in Ontario and Manitoba can survive only in places where they enjoy complete protection from these predators during calving. Cows in these populations swim to islands far from shore in large lakes to give birth, and return to the mainland only when the calves are well advanced.

In many parts of Alaska and the Yukon, grizzly bears also prey on caribou calves. These bears, which are normally too slow to catch adult caribou except perhaps cripples, can easily chase down newborn calves or females incapacitated while giving birth. On some calving grounds, bears kill more calves than do wolves. They hunt by charging through an area in which cows with young calves have concentrated. The bears substitute endurance and persistence for speed; a calf that initially can outdistance a grizzly may succumb after the bear pursues it for a mile or more, driving through slushy snowdrifts and smashing aside willow tangles. During such a chase the grizzly puts hundreds of cows to flight. In the confusion and panic, many calves become separated from their mothers and abandoned. They make easy prey for the bear later on.

Caribou will defend their young against smaller carnivores by

kicking at the predators or threatening them with their antlers. Arctic foxes are often seen near females with newborn calves. Although the foxes may be seeking the afterbirth, they are certainly capable of killing an undefended calf, for arctic foxes regularly kill the lambs of domestic sheep in Iceland. Cows have been seen to defend their calves successfully against wolverines in Canada, although in Scandinavia European wolverines kill many wild reindeer calves.

Another enemy of young calves is the lynx. In Newfoundland, where wolves were exterminated, lynx became a major cause of mortality among woodland caribou calves. The lynx stalk and attack young calves in the forested calving grounds when snowshoe hares, their normal prey, are scarce. Even if the calf escapes the attack, it often dies later of *Pasteurella* infection introduced by the lynx's bite.

The golden eagles that nest abundantly in Alaska and the Yukon also prey on caribou calves. Attacks by eagles may explain why calves in Alaska and the Yukon sometimes nurse standing directly under the females; this nursing position is rare in herds from areas where eagles are absent.

Between the ever-present threats of predators and the rigorous climate of the northern lands, the calves' first few days and weeks of life hold a multitude of dangers. Many calves do not survive to join the immense herds that travel through the brief explosive flowering of the summer tundra.

CALVING PHOTOGRAPHS

Pages 46-47: Newborn calf, Bathurst herd calving grounds, Northwest Territories.

Page 51: A small band of pregnant cows travels across the open cottongrass plains of the Porcupine herd calving grounds near the Jago River, Alaska.

Page 52: Water from the melting snow runs in sheets over the ground, Bathurst herd calving grounds, Northwest Territories.

Page 54: Cow that has just given birth, Delta herd calving grounds, Alaska.

Page 55: Throughout the first hours after birth, the cow devotes her attention to licking and smelling the calf. This is part of the formation of the bond between mother and young. Delta herd calving grounds, Alaska.

Page 56: The cow devotes almost constant attention to her calf during its first two days of life, learning its characteristics so that she can distinguish it from the thousands in the great summer herds. Delta herd calving grounds, Alaska.

Page 57: The cow relies above all on scent for positive identification of her young, although later on she learns its voice and may even be able to distinguish its appearance. Porcupine herd calving grounds, near the Jago River, Alaska.

Pages 58-59: Within a few hours after birth, the calf can stumble along behind its mother for long distances if the two are disturbed. Porcupine herd calving grounds, near the Jago River, Alaska.

Pages 60-61: Male snow goose stands guard as his mate incubates her eggs, Bathurst herd calving grounds, Northwest Territories.

Pages 62-63: Soon after giving birth, cows lead their calves into the company of other females and young. Bathurst herd calving grounds, Northwest Territories.

Page 65 (upper): Red phalarope, one of the scores of species of shorebirds that flock to the Arctic to nest each summer, taking advantage of the short burst of productivity, Southampton Island, Northwest Territories.

Page 65 (middle): Cottongrass flowers that appear on many calving grounds, even before the snow is gone, provide concentrated nutrients for the nursing cows. Porcupine herd calving grounds, near the Jago River, Alaska.

Page 65 (lower): Cow in labour, Porcupine herd calving grounds, near the Jago River, Alaska.

Page 66 (upper): Red-backed vole, one of several species of small tundra animals.

Page 66 (middle): Lapland longspur after a two-day snowstorm, Porcupine herd calving grounds, near the Jago River, Alaska.

Page 66 (lower): Soon after giving birth, the cow sheds the placenta and eats it; hormones from the afterbirth stimulate her production of milk. Here the wobbly youngster is already searching for the udder to nurse. Delta herd calving grounds, Alaska.

Page 67: Still unsteady on its feet, a newborn calf can be readily recognized by its hunched posture and oddly bent hind legs. Porcupine herd calving grounds, near the Jago River, Alaska.

Page 68 (left): Cows become extremely wary after the birth of their calves. This cow has detected an intruder and is already standing in the alarm posture, calling the calf to get up and follow her away. The calf's head is just visible among the tussocks about fifteen feet in front of her. Porcupine herd calving grounds, near the Jago River, Alaska.

Page 68 (right): Long-tailed jaeger flies in to feed on a dead calf, Delta herd calving grounds, Alaska.

Summer
The great herds

Summer movements of the Porcupine herd

It was midnight but the sun had not set. Nor would it dip below the horizon for several more weeks; for it was mid-summer and this land lay hundreds of miles north of the Arctic Circle. The Brooks Range loomed blue and massive on the southern skyline, the snow-tipped peaks burnished with golden light. Towering cumulus clouds reared higher yet above the summits. From the mountains, vast undulating plains of cottongrass ran down to the Beaufort Sea. Although it was the first week of July, the sea was still locked in ice.

In all directions, as far as the eye could see, caribou grazed slowly and peacefully on the golden plains. In the stillness the sounds of the herd carried far over the land: hooves splashing in the sedgy ponds, cows calling to their calves. Virtually all the females and calves of the Porcupine herd, eighty thousand strong, were assembled here on the coastal tundra between the Jago and Hulahula rivers on Alaska's North Slope.

The gathering of these caribou had occurred gradually. The migrating cows had reached the coastal plain of the northern Yukon and northeastern Alaska in late May, and there had given birth to their calves. Then during the ensuing weeks, the females and their young had gradually drifted west, travelling slowly, a few miles a day. As they moved, bands had come together into larger and larger groups. The first animals had reached the Jago River by mid-June and then slowed their movements. Continuing arrivals swelled the numbers. Now, on all the vast coastal plain stretching from the Mackenzie Delta to Prudhoe Bay, this area of perhaps five hundred square miles was virtually the only one that contained caribou.

The animals were scattered in many loose groups, each numbering from a few hundred to several thousand. Cows and calves grazed together in pairs. A calf would push its face in close beside its mother's muzzle as she fed, to learn by sight and smell what she selected to eat. Although the young ones were already getting much of their nourishment by grazing and could, if necessary, live entirely on plant material, most of them still nursed as well. Producing the rich milk for their offspring, so soon after the demands of pregnancy and the exertion of spring migration, had reduced the cows' physical condition to its ebb for the year. They appeared even more gaunt than at the end of the spring migration. The ribs of many showed clearly through their worn coats, and ragged patches were appearing on the necks and sides of some animals where last year's hair had been shed and the dark new coat was growing in. Many calves were also changing colour, the reddish-brown hue of birth giving way to the tawny grey they would carry during the rest of the year.

The next day the wind shifted to the southeast, blowing across the warm land rather than from the icy ocean. The temperature rose. That morning the thin whine of the year's first mosquitoes was heard. As the day progressed, a pattern of movement developed among the throngs on the plains: the caribou were drifting into the wind. As they travelled, groups merged. By evening the entire population had assembled into two huge herds massed along the Jago River. Each occupied no more than a few square miles of tundra, and within those vortices of life tens of thousands of caribou milled and grazed fitfully.

The wind died as the sun dipped towards the horizon. The mosquitoes swarmed around the caribou. In a single day the insects had reached pestilent proportions. Like so many events in the arctic summer, their emergence had occurred explosively. The annual season of torment had begun. For the next month no warm-blooded creature would be safe from the scourge, except on windy days or during cold rainy weather. They would attack the white downy young of peregrine falcons and eagles in their nests on cliffs, pester wolf and fox pups at the mouths of their dens, and continually attack the caribou. Under the onslaught of the insects, the caribou headed north to the coast. Here the nearby sea ice cooled the air, and the bare gravel of the river delta offered fewer resting places for the mosquitoes than did the vegetation of the tundra.

The next morning found the caribou in their thousands lying and standing on the gravel among the maze of braided channels and ponds. Along the stream channels there remained patches of thick ice, formed during periods of overflow in the winter. Many caribou sought refuge by lying on the ice; some even waded out into the ponds and sea water. But the delta offered little food for the animals: the herd soon had to move inland to feed. As the sun rose in the sky, the warm wind sprang up again from the east. As they grazed, the caribou travelled into the wind to obtain some relief from the relentless mosquitoes. The movement of the great summer herds had begun.

The mass of caribou no longer acted as individuals. The herd had taken on a life and an energy of its own. Like a single giant organism it advanced over the land, along a front up to several miles wide, driven by the harassment of the mosquitoes. During spells of calm, humid weather – ideal conditions for the insects – the caribou were driven to a frenzy. They bunched together so tightly that

from a distance they appeared a solid mass. They trotted frantically into the slightest breeze, trying to keep the clouds of mosquitoes off the sensitive parts of their faces: eyes, ears, lips, and nostrils. The beleaguered animals tossed their heads, snorted, flicked their ears, and shook themselves as though shedding water after a swim. Here and there an individual stopped for a moment within the flow of the herd to scratch an ear or an antler with a hind hoof, or to bite at its flanks. The caribou covered the ground quickly, heads down, snatching mouthfuls of vegetation on the move. From within the confusion came the grunting of cows calling to their calves and the continual bleating of lost youngsters. And from the thousands of passing hooves came a distinct clicking sound. In this way the herd advanced, in stops and starts, snorting, shaking, and harried, each caribou a part of the multitude but alone with its insect tormentors.

The vast plains over which the herd travelled appeared a drab greenish brown, the colour of the cottongrass and other sedges that dominated the vegetation. But against this dull background many small jewel-like flowers were in bloom. Marsh marigolds brightened the edges of small tundra ponds. On drier places grew mountain avens, pink clumps of moss campion, and arctic poppies whose golden petals waved in the slightest breeze. And when the sun dipped towards the horizon, mile after mile of cottongrass heads nodded in the evening light. The earliest blossoms like the bright purple saxifrage and the delicate-appearing but hardy pasque flowers were almost gone, remaining only where the snow had lingered late. Dwarf arctic willows sported red-tipped catkins, miniature versions of the familiar pussy willows of spring. These tiny shrubs provided the bulk of the caribou's diet at this season. Among the cottongrass tussocks, woolly louseworts thrust up their odd fuzzy spikes covered with pink flowers. The caribou sought these blossoms for food as well.

The plains were also alive with birds. Every pond and wetland was the centre of activity for a host of shorebirds that had come to the Arctic to raise their broods during summer's brief explosion of productivity. Northern phalaropes twirled and bobbed on the surface, sending concentric ripples across the still water as they fed on small invertebrates. Semi-palmated sandpipers and dunlins scurried along the sedgy pond margins, their nests hidden in the tundra vegetation nearby. A few of the sandpiper broods had begun to hatch, and the precocious rust and grey chicks were already snapping up the abundant insects that would nourish their rapid growth. The same insects that tormented the caribou were the food of life for the small birds. On larger ponds red-throated or

arctic loons were nesting, each female incubating her two brown-spotted eggs. Whistling swans and brooding pintails shared the ponds with them. Graceful long-tailed jaegers made their nests on the tundra, and if the caribou approached their territories, the birds dived at them and harassed them until the caribou turned away. Smaller, less aggressive birds – the sandpipers, longspurs, and even ptarmigan – were not so fortunate. Those whose nests lay in the path of the hurrying herd were powerless to stop the destruction of their eggs and broods beneath the avalanche of hooves.

As the huge herd of cows and calves continued eastward along the coastal plain, they now began to meet groups of bulls, still moving west along the same routes that the cows had followed weeks earlier. The bulls mingled with the females and young and reversed their direction of travel. By the sixth of July the caribou had covered sixty miles and were almost to the Kongakut River.

The tundra shimmered with heat waves under the afternoon sun. The air vibrated with the barely audible humming of myriad flying insects, experiencing their brief moment of life. Along the river bank an arctic ground squirrel bounded back and forth between its burrow and a succulent patch of vegetation. Three arctic terns screeched and dived at one another as they hunted over the glittering river channels. A semi-palmated plover pattered and pecked along the silty beach. Except for these small points of movement, the tundra appeared static and empty beneath the vault of the sky.

Then a movement appeared in the mirage. At first it seemed nothing more than a darkening on the horizon, but soon the disturbance resolved itself into an advancing herd of caribou, stretched and distorted in the heat. The huge-antlered mirage advanced, shimmered, grew larger. Thousands upon thousands of caribou were approaching. They covered the land until the very ground itself seemed to move and flow with life. Rutted trails, worn deep in the tundra by countless hooves of summers past, led to this traditional river crossing, foretelling what must happen.

A stream of caribou broke off to the north, parallel to the river, and the herd swung to follow. But a countermovement started south, and those going north slowed and stopped. They retraced their steps. The herd appeared hesitant and vacillating. From the middle of the mass, still others continued towards the river.

A few dozen animals finally reached the river and started grazing along the bank. Thousands more pressed in close behind. Then, suddenly, the caribou at the river's edge whirled and stampeded back towards the others. Within minutes the entire herd had thundered away, almost to the horizon.

The caribou took an hour to work their way back to the river. Again small groups of animals reached the bank and fed nervously, glancing across the water as the main herd closed in behind them. Then they made another precipitate retreat. Once more all lay quiet along the river while the herd milled in the distance.

When the caribou advanced for the third time, they came on more quickly and appeared more determined. A cow followed closely by her calf led a line of perhaps a hundred animals to the crossing place. The herd followed but hung back as the cow hesitated at the water's edge. She sniffed, glanced behind, then across the channel, and stepped into the water. She waded slowly, slipping on the rounded cobbles in the stream bed. Her calf followed closely, also stumbling and splashing until it reached swimming depth. The group on shore watched their progress as they smoothly breasted the channel and lunged out on the other side in a flurry of spray. Without a backward glance, the pair shook themselves and trotted away. The throng on the opposite bank stood watching for a moment and then suddenly turned and retreated yet again.

The sun was low when the great herd made its fourth approach to the river. This time they were travelling so fast that clouds of dust roiled the air. The caribou massed on the bank, the sun lighting up the velvet on the antlers of the gathered bulls. The advancing thousands pressed tightly together. Tension hung palpably in the air. Ripples of anticipation raced through the herd. Finally, a cow and a calf waded into the stream. Others followed quickly, then more, and more. At last the hesitancy was broken. The living flood poured into the river.

For the next hour the herd massed, splashed, waded, and swam. Wave after wave of caribou trotted to the water and, urged on by the pressure from behind, plunged in. At times their bodies pressed so closely together that it seemed the animals squeezed in the centre must surely be crushed or drowned. A turmoil of grunting, wheezing, and splashing filled the air. The heavy odour of hot, struggling animals hung over the scene. Bands of bulls crossed together, their antlers sticking up like a floating forest. A calf separated from its mother swam gamely

alongside massive bulls in the surge and crush, its small body contrasting with their size and power.

Now and then some imagined danger stopped the flow of caribou as they reached the opposite shore. They stood irresolutely in the shallows or at the river's edge, glancing from side to side and back across the water they had just crossed. These sudden halts forced those still swimming to mill and thrash, piling up in the current. Some even turned around and tried to fight their way back, heightening the turmoil. In the confusion many animals were swept downstream.

At the peak of the crossing the surge to reach the river grew so strong that two new points of entry were established. Now three lines of swimmers steadily stemmed the river. The great herd crossed continuously for an hour. Then, as abruptly as it had begun, the seemingly endless flood of caribou was over. No more animals advanced out of the golden distance to replace those entering the river. The last swimmers slid through the water, clambered out, shook quickly, and trotted after the vanishing herd. The horizon stood empty.

Two calves wandered along the far shore bleating for their mothers. A small band of bewildered yearlings stood looking back at the river for a few moments before hurrying away. This place, which moments before had seemed the pulsing centre of all life, was now just another undistinguished piece of tundra. The midnight sun shone on the emptiness. A few longspurs and tree sparrows fluttered about, whistling sadly, their nests destroyed and their world trampled beyond recognition by the hooves of the vanishing herd. Soon the winds would blow away the primordial smell that still hung in the air. The hair floating like straw in the eddies would drift away with the current. Then only the trails would remember the exuberance of life that had passed this way.

After crossing the Kongakut, the caribou climbed into the foothills. During the next four days their journey continued eastward through these high valleys and rocky slopes. Here they met more big bulls. Like the others, these bulls were absorbed by the huge herds of cows and immature animals.

The weather remained clear and hot, and under these conditions the caribou fell into a distinct pattern of daily activity. In the warmest part of the day the animals massed together on ridge tops. Here the wind and dry heat kept the mosquitoes to a tolerable level. The caribou took advantage of the lack of harassment to rest and feed. In the evenings, as the air cooled, the mosquitoes swarmed out of the vegetation. Then the herd descended from its daytime refuge.

As they moved through the open valleys and broad slopes, the caribou spread out over a wide front, but where the mountain watersheds constricted to narrow passes they formed long files. Often the herd straggled out over five miles or more, as they ascended one steep, narrowing valley and spilled over into the next.

The caribou's walk appeared slow and easy, but actually covered the rugged terrain at four or five miles an hour. They generally travelled steadily for an hour or two, then stopped to feed in some particularly lush pasture. In these high shaded drainages the growth and development of plants lagged behind those on the coast. The buds, new leaves, and flowers were therefore still rich with concentrated nutrients. The caribou sought the leaves of the felt leaf willow, the buds of cottongrass, the flowers of the lupine. Their milling hooves cut and smashed the vegetation into the moist soil. Stream banks became rutted with muddy trails bearing the imprint of thousands of hooves. The animals travelled in this way each night, covering about fifteen miles. Before the sun had dried the dew on the grass and flowers, they climbed once again to an exposed ridge and settled down to spend another day.

Early in the evening of July tenth the herd reached the Malcolm River. Rather than crossing, they fed along its banks where it coursed out of the foothills onto the coastal plain. They milled for several hours before splashing across the wide braided channel in the early morning mist. Then they stopped and grazed for the rest of the day on the plain between the Malcolm and the Firth, the next river to the east.

As the caribou were getting underway that evening, a female grizzly bear followed by two small cubs suddenly appeared over a knoll and galloped into the herd. In such open terrain her attack had little hope of success. Nevertheless, the sow charged about among the massed caribou for several minutes, perhaps hoping to find a cripple or to force some animal to make a mistake in the confusion. Confident in their superior speed, many caribou did not even stand up until the bear approached within a hundred yards. The cubs were beside themselves with excitement. They raced close behind their mother, then stopped and stood up on their hind legs, peering in all directions at the swirl of movement around them. The smell of the massed prey assailed their sensitive noses. After a few charges, the sow accepted the hopelessness of the chase and broke off.

Calling her cubs, she ambled away, crossed a small stream, and began to search along the bank for ground squirrel burrows, which offered easier pickings than the fleet caribou.

The bear's attack split the herd: a smaller vanguard of several thousand animals continued eastward, but the bulk of the caribou turned southeast. The two groups travelled separately throughout the night, but rejoined the next morning on the banks of the Firth River.

That day was warm and humid. The mosquitoes had reached their height of virulence. The caribou stood packed tightly together enduring the onslaught until suddenly, in part of the herd, some animals began to buck and run. The disturbance spread rapidly until the entire herd stampeded outwards from the centre. From a distance the herd appeared to explode. Grunting and wheezing from the distraught animals could be heard for several miles. When they stampeded, the sound was like the roar of distant wind. Then gradually the animals calmed down and moved back into a dense herd again until another panic struck. This performance was repeated throughout the day. After each rush stray calves and their mothers could be seen searching for one another around the edges of the herd. The throng of caribou remained massed on the bank, enduring the torture of the mosquitoes until evening. Then they moved south upriver for almost twenty miles into the mountains. As it travelled, the herd split into three groups. Morning found each resting on a different ridge.

The three herds crossed the river separately on the evening of July thirteenth and climbed into the British Mountains to the east. There their routes diverged; each pursued its own way through these mountains that separate the Arctic Coast from the Old Crow Flats. Compared with the coastal plain, these high drainages were silent and lifeless. The landscape was enlivened only by a few wandering tattlers protesting the invasion of their nesting territories, and an occasional ptarmigan scurrying away with her brood. The sound of frost-shattered rock stirred by tens of thousands of hooves echoed off the surrounding slopes, as the caribou crossed the heads of the valleys.

The dangers of migration were taking a heavy toll of calves. Sheer exhaustion and the persistent attacks of insects had weakened many of the animals. Some had drowned at river crossings; others had been injured during their travels through the rugged terrain. In the hills wolves were more common than on the coastal plain. They hunted from ambush, darting out of the willows as the caribou crossed small streams. The animals at the rear of the herd piled into those in front, who were often unaware of the danger and panic behind them. With their escape thus blocked, many fell victim to the predators. Wolves often killed several calves in a single attack. Grizzlies also ambushed an occasional calf and fed on those that had died from accidents along the way.

As the summer migration continued through the British and Barn mountains, groups continually broke apart and rejoined. On the eighteenth of July the first of the several groups of caribou reached the headwaters of the Blow River. Here they left the mountains and turned southeast. The last part of their summer travels took them across the open rolling plains past Bonnet Lake to the headwaters of the Driftwood River, at the far eastern edge of the Old Crow Flats.

They were now two hundred miles from the Jago River where the great herd had first formed, but they had covered perhaps twice that distance on their meandering route. Several large groups wandered around the head of the Driftwood River until the end of July. Then, in a matter of days, the caribou scattered in all directions.

Most headed west, crossing the Old Crow Flats and into the high hills across the Alaskan border. Others moved east, climbing the slopes of the Richardson Mountains and then north to the edge of the Mackenzie River Delta. Still others travelled south to Rat Pass, the Bell River, and beyond. A few went back into the Barn Mountains. Where tens of thousands had journeyed together a week before, now there were groups of a hundred here, a dozen there, lone bulls grazing peacefully in the ever-shortening days. The time of the great herds was at an end.

The summer massing of the caribou on the barren-lands is a spectacle to rival anything in the living world. Virtually all the members of a herd may come together: groups over 100,000 strong have been observed in some years. As these huge gatherings move off on their summer journey, they flow like a geological force across the tundra. Thousands of sharp hooves carve trails into the soil and even into rocks of mountain passes. The din of grunting animals and clicking hooves sounds for miles across the barren-lands. They move restlessly, for such a throng would quickly deplete the forage anywhere it stopped.

From these great summer herds spring the legends of uncountable millions of caribou, the myth of the Arctic's fabulous productivity. No explorer could fail to be deeply moved and astounded by a jostling, milling herd stretching to the horizon. The sight and sound and smell of such a prodigious overflowing of life are beyond experience, almost beyond imagination. There is no way to estimate the numbers of caribou from the ground on flat tundra. Ten thousand become a hundred thousand in the telling, a hundred thousand become millions, and so the story grows. A hunter observing the passing of such herds must believe the supply of game to be limitless.

But those who witness these annual spectacles are often unaware that they are seeing virtually all the caribou from an immense area of country. Similar abundance cannot be attributed to adjacent areas. There are no more animals just over the next hill. When the Bathurst caribou mass on the ridges overlooking the inlet that gives them their name, the other 200,000 square miles of their range are virtually empty. These herds, overwhelming as they may be, contain all the caribou in each region.

Biologists refer to the great herds of summer as post-calving aggregations. As the name implies, they begin to form soon after the birth of the young. After a day or two of isolation, cows bring their newborn into the company of other cows and calves. Yearlings left behind during spring migration, or driven off by the cows when their new calves were born, rejoin the herd to swell the numbers further. Loose assemblies of several thousand have usually formed by the latter half of June, and tightly massed groups numbering tens of thousands are on the move by early July.

Normally each herd forms several post-calving aggregations, ranging in size from a few hundred animals to many thousands. The number and structure of the individual groups change from day to day as they break up and re-form over and over while they travel. The largest assemblies, those numbering 50,000 or more, often form where terrain channels or impedes several smaller groups, for example in mountain passes or at river crossings.

The bulls, which have remained segregated from the cows during spring migration and the calving period, also form large herds in July. Sometimes such herds, consisting almost entirely of mature bulls, roam the tundra without ever joining the cows. But if the cows, calves, and yearlings retrace the routes they used in approaching the calving grounds, they will usually meet up with the bulls who follow these routes several weeks later. Even when all age groups and both sexes travel together, they do not mix randomly. The mature bulls often remain in one part of the herd; yearlings and juveniles tend to group on the periphery.

The formation of the summer herds each year coincides with the emergence of mosquitoes. The caribou of the Porcupine herd, for example, are scattered over many hundreds of square miles of the coastal tundra in late June before the mosquitoes have hatched. Then, immediately following the first appearance of mosquitoes, the caribou come together into one or two enormous herds and begin to travel east, into the prevailing

wind. They remain in these aggregations of many thousands throughout the month or so during which the insects are virulent.

The tundra provides ideal breeding habitat for mosquitoes. Although little rain or snow falls in most of the Arctic, what water there is stays on the surface because the underlying ground remains permanently frozen. Only the upper few feet of the tundra soil thaw each summer. Below that the permafrost prevents the water from sinking in, and it collects in every low spot and depression. These small stagnant pools, warmed by the continuous sunlight of the arctic summer, become productive hatcheries. Mosquitoes swarm out by the millions. In the central barrens the many fast-flowing streams also produce plagues of blackflies.

The caribou's behaviour at this season is dominated by their attempts to find relief from mosquitoes. When days are warm and calm, flies torture the animals, swarming about them, concentrating where the hair is thin: on the muzzle and around the eyes and ears. The more numerous and active the insects, the larger the aggregation of caribou, the more tightly they bunch, and the more restlessly they travel. To keep the pests off their faces, the caribou move into the wind whenever possible. In hilly or mountainous terrain they huddle on windswept ridges. On flat tundra even an esker or a knoll may offer a little extra breeze. Caribou on the coastal plain of Alaska travel to the Arctic Ocean to enjoy the cold wind blowing off the ice; some even wade into the frigid water. On the central barrens in Canada herds mass on the shores of large lakes, which remain ice-covered well into July. Snow patches and areas of overflow ice on rivers are avidly sought as resting places because the snow cools the air above, inhibiting the activity of insects.

On the Arctic Islands and in the far northeastern part of the Northwest Territories, mosquitoes and blackflies are less numerous. Here caribou do not mass in large herds; rather, they spend the summer in groups of half a dozen or less, or even as lone individuals. Snow patches constitute the usual refuge for these small summer groups. One July, while studying the caribou near Wager Bay in the Northwest Territories, I did a reconnaissance flight along a river appropriately named the Snowbank. Everywhere beneath the deeply incised banks the winter winds had packed huge drifts that remained despite the summer heat. I saw caribou seeking relief from mosquitoes on virtually every snowbank: a cow and calf here, two yearlings on the next, a lone bull on the third, and so on for many miles. The caribou may even frequent sand dunes or gravel deltas of rivers, because these areas devoid of plants offer fewer places for mosquitoes to hide and breed than does the wet vegetation of the tundra.

When insects harass the caribou severely, the animals find little peace to feed or chew their cuds. Their feeding rate drops, and they forage on the move, snatching a mouthful here or there. Panic may spread through the herds as the caribou are tormented beyond the limits of endurance. During such stampedes calves become separated from their mothers, and in extreme instances the frantic animals may even trample one another to death.

Caribou take advantage of any respite offered by cool windy weather to feed and rest. I saw a particularly clear instance of the effects of weather on a post-calving aggregation one hot and humid evening while I was camped near Kaminuriak Lake. A couple of miles away a herd of about 10,000 caribou was being driven wild by the clouds of mosquitoes. The animals raced back and forth at the edge of the lake, running for half a mile in one direction, milling for a few minutes, then dashing off again the opposite way. Finally the herd started trotting frantically along the shore towards my camp. As they were passing within a hundred yards of the tent, a strong wind suddenly sprang up. The mosquitoes vanished instantly. The temperature dropped from shirt-sleeve weather to almost freezing in minutes. I put on a sweater and a down jacket and wished that I had mittens as I sat watching the caribou through binoculars. It was as though a soothing balm had been poured over the harried animals. They slowed and stopped. Many immediately dropped to the ground and curled up to rest; others began grazing placidly. Calves nursed and then lay quietly beside their mothers. The sense of relief among the animals was tangible. The herd remained by the camp all night, but next day, when the warm humid weather returned, they grouped up again and trotted away.

The caribou's efforts to escape the insect pestilence cost them precious energy at a time when their reserves are already low. Each animal may lose up to a quart of blood a week during the peak of the insect season. These additional energy losses force the condition of the cows to its lowest ebb of the year, and slow the growth of calves and young animals.

The caribou that travel the tundra or mountains near the end of the mosquito season are a ragged and exhausted lot. Their coats are tattered where large patches of the light-coloured winter hair have fallen out. All the animals are growing antlers. Those of the cows and calves are merely fuzzy stubs, but the mature bulls sport already massive antlers, still tender and flexible beneath the grey velvet. The growth of new hair and antlers requires energy and large quantities of minerals, protein, and other nutrients. Cows have already used up most of their stored fat to produce and nurse their calves. Calves and yearlings are always lean; their energy goes exclusively for growth. Only the bulls are in reasonably good condition in July.

Fortunately, the caribou's summer forage consists mainly of new sprouts and buds as well as flowers — plant parts particularly rich in energy, minerals, and protein. The routes followed by the post-calving herds may actually be chosen to take the caribou into terrain that provides both relief from insects, and vegetation that is high in nutrients. They may also supplement their diet by eating the soil at natural mineral licks containing elements such as sulphur, sodium, and chlorine.

Summer holds other hazards for the great herds. Their routes carry them back into areas where denning wolves are an ever-present threat. In fact, it has been suggested that one of the reasons the caribou form large aggregations soon after calving may be as a defence against predators. A large herd may make it difficult for a predator to single out and concentrate on one target; a large band may also be more likely to detect danger than would a lone caribou. Since caribou in the dense aggregations occupy only a tiny part of the herd's total range at any one time, they are exposed to fewer predators than if they scattered over large tracts of country. This holds especially true when the predators occupy fixed home ranges, as wolves and grizzly bears are known to do.

On the other hand, caribou in very large herds often seem unwary, especially if insects are bothering them. If only a few individuals in a herd detect danger, their behaviour may not be sufficient to alarm the rest. Many times I have been completely surrounded by a moving herd and the animals that saw me merely turned aside; the majority remained unaware of my presence. Often I have walked to within a hundred yards of a huge summer aggregation and only the animals on the periphery assumed the alarm posture or moved away. Confusion in a large group may actually work against the caribou rather than against the predator. Calves in particular become disoriented when a herd takes flight, and fail to see a wolf until it appears from behind another caribou. The young animals tend to pace themselves with the group, rather than sprinting at the proper moment to escape.

My experiences suggest that wolves have little trouble catching caribou from the summer herds, especially the vulnerable calves. During the passage of the Bathurst caribou in July 1980, I witnessed a drama that unfolds countless times each year, with infinite variations. From a high ridge I was watching several thousand animals that had just left a patch of snow and were grazing across a broad green slope leading down to Bathurst Lake. A lone white wolf appeared, sniffing across the well-tracked snow that the caribou had just abandoned, and stood looking at the horde spread out below. As the wolf trotted towards the caribou, I suddenly became aware of a single cow leading her strayed calf back to the group. The wolf must have sensed the vulnerability of the pair, for he loped down to cut off the cow from her companions. I heard the roar of hooves as the wolf charged the main herd, stampeding them further away. Then he turned to concentrate on his chosen quarry: the cow and calf. He kept himself between them and the safety of the herd as he trotted forward. When he finally made his move, he seemed to know that the isolated animals would head for the group. As the cow raced in a wide circle with the calf sprinting at her heels, the wolf cut across this arc and drew alongside. The small animal had no chance as the wolf, three times its size, reached down to grab it by the neck. The dead calf looked no more substantial than a large rabbit, as the wolf carried it dangling from his jaws to a nearby outcrop. I watched him stop to tear briefly at the kill before he disappeared.

The next day I hiked to the place where I had last seen the wolf with the dead calf. There I found the carcass. The wolf had eaten only the tongue and a small portion of the innards. During the next few days I came across four more dead calves within a mile of the first, all with just the brain or tongue eaten, the abdomen opened slightly. Other biologists have reported similar incidents of wolves making multiple kills of calves and abandoning the carcasses essentially uneaten. I also saw many abandoned calves and small groups of stragglers, including several limping animals. Such "rearguard" animals, which are always to be found in the wake of the summer herds, constitute easy prey for wolves.

Stampedes and panics caused by insect harassment and the attacks of predators are two factors contributing to the constant splitting and rejoining of the summer herds. Lakes or ridges may also divide the flow of migration. The herd is constantly changing; the animals mill together as they feed; females search for errant calves; groups of yearlings dart from the herd to investigate anything that attracts their curiosity.

It seems inconceivable that caribou could learn to recognize other individuals, or that there could be any social structure in these turbulent, ever-changing herds. Yet there are hints that smaller groups exist within the apparent chaos. The evidence comes mainly from studies of marked animals. Radio transmitters were placed on twenty-seven females of the Kaminuriak herd during their spring migration in April 1970, and the radio signals were used to locate them at intervals throughout the spring and summer. The cows produced calves normally and joined the post-calving aggregations. These groups travelled hundreds of miles across the tundra during July, and several times fragmented into smaller groups and recombined in various ways. Despite this shuffling, certain of the marked animals were seen together repeatedly and, after separating, these animals returned to the same groups. Similar observations have been made with caribou captured at water crossings during the summer and marked with ear-tags. In many instances animals tagged from the same group were still together when shot by hunters a year or more later.

Such evidence of long-standing associations between individual caribou has led to the speculation that caribou herds might be composed of smaller social units that stay together throughout the winter. Possibly the huge summer aggregations serve to bring the caribou together, so that winter band members may locate each other again after the spring migration and dispersal for calving.

The caribou cannot journey far in any direction during their summer travels without crossing a river or confronting a lake that they must find their way around. Vast regions of the barren-lands are as much water as land. The lakes and rivers that served as frozen highways for the migrating caribou in spring become obstacles to be crossed or circumvented in the summer. Contwoyto Lake, stretching over seventy-five miles from southeast to northwest, constitutes such a barrier to the Bathurst herd. When the caribou reach the lake, they change course and travel along the shore until they find a way around the north or south end. They must cross the many rivers flowing into the lake, and long bays extending inland. Deep rutted trails scored into the tundra by the hooves of many generations lead to the best crossings at the narrows and shallow spots. I have stood in trails worn eighteen inches deep into the soil near a water crossing at Contwoyto Lake.

Such ancestral trails mark the summer passage on the ranges of all large caribou herds. They lead to crossing places that have been used for centuries, perhaps millennia, and are well known to the native peoples. In times past, hunters camped at these traditional crossings, awaiting the arrival of the herds. By spearing from kayaks they could kill hundreds of animals as the caribou swam the crossing. Piles of bones and antlers and the rock cairns used to cache the meat still mark the scenes of these bygone hunts.

Caribou are excellent swimmers, the best among the deer family. Their air-filled coats give them buoyancy, and their broad hollow hooves provide ample surface area for propulsion. They swim holding their heads high, backs and shoulders completely out of the water, and their stubby white tails standing straight up. Usually they enter the water and swim in single file, the calves trailing close behind their mothers. But if a very large herd is crossing, hundreds of animals splash into the water in a wide band. When undisturbed, the caribou swim at three or four miles an hour; if frightened or chased, they can manage spurts of six or seven miles an hour.

Despite their proficiency in the water and the numerous swims that they make each summer, the caribou approach crossings warily and often appear hesitant to enter the water. Many groups may pile up at a crossing, thus creating huge but short-lived herds that last only until the crossing is finally made. A herd may approach the water and withdraw several times, grazing restively in the intervals. Tension and uneasiness build with each retreat. Almost always a mature cow leads the approaches, her calf tagging close at her heels. A different cow may be in the vanguard each time, until finally one takes the plunge and the herd pours across in her wake. On gaining the opposite shore the caribou race out of the water, as though anxious to get away from the crossing site.

The caribou's nervousness probably arises from their sense of vulnerability both in the water and when massed at the water's edge. Wolves haunt the crossing sites, hiding in the willows that grow along the stream banks. With the caribou's escape blocked by the water in one direction and by the tightly packed herd in the other, wolves can often make an easy kill in the confusion. Most of the wolf kills that I have witnessed occurred at or near stream crossings, and at more than one crossing place I have found several dead calves, all bearing the characteristic wounds on the head and neck that indicated they had been killed by wolves. The crossings themselves may be dangerous. Many of the rivers of the barrens are swift-flowing, with fearsome rapids and falls. Injury and drowning at water crossings are probably the major forms of accidental death in barren-ground caribou. The sound of riffles and rapids attracts the caribou, for they usually find shallow water there; but if they enter the river in fast water above a powerful set of rapids, they can be swept away and injured or drowned in the maelstrom. Such accidents occur regularly on the rapids of the Hanbury River where the Beverly herd crosses each summer. Scavengers gather there to feed on the carrion: wolverines, wolves, barren-ground grizzlies, ravens, and herring gulls. The shallow braided streams on the coastal plain in Alaska and the Yukon are not as dangerous as those of the barrens, but the larger ones, such as the Kongakut and the Firth, claim some lives. Caribou drown at other seasons too, especially in autumn when rivers and lakes freeze up. The migrating animals appear remarkably unafraid of thin ice, and often fall through.

The many hazards of the summer migration take a heavy toll of calves. As the smallest and weakest members of the herds, they are the most vulnerable to the attacks of mosquitoes, the most susceptible to injury in stampedes, the most likely to drown. Predators single them out. Calves that have strayed from their mothers or become separated during stampedes have little chance of survival. In some herds thirty to fifty per cent of the new generation may die during the month of July, falling victim to a variety of dangers and stresses. More calves are lost during the brief summer than at any other period of the year, except in some years when violent storms on the calving grounds kill many newborn.

At the end of July or early August the large herds suddenly disperse. The break-up coincides, more or less, with the disappearance of the mosquitoes, which have completed their life cycle for another year. At about that time two other insect parasites – the warble fly and the nose bot – reach their peak of abundance. The extreme reactions that the caribou exhibit to escape these flies likely contribute to breaking up the post-calving herds.

The warble fly looks like a small yellow and black bumblebee. It lays its eggs on the fur of the caribou, usually on the legs or abdomen, and when the larvae hatch they burrow under the skin and migrate to the back and rump. Here they encapsulate and cut a breathing hole through the caribou's skin. Infestations are often heavy; caribou commonly carry more than a hundred larvae, and individual animals infested with over 2000 of these parasites have been recorded. The pests grow and develop through the autumn and winter, and by spring have reached a length of half an inch. In May and June they burrow through the skin and drop to the ground to pupate. The exit holes remain in the skin well into July, and native peoples therefore find summer caribou skins worthless for clothing.

The nose bot is ovo-viviparous; it places live larvae in the nostrils of the caribou. These migrate through the nasal passages to establish themselves at the entrance to the throat. By spring the growing larvae form a mass so large that it may interfere with the animal's breathing. During the later stages of spring migration, caribou are often heard coughing, as though trying to rid themselves of the pests.

The caribou react differently to attacks by these flies than to mosquito harassment. Both warble flies and nose bots are such strong fliers that the animals cannot avoid them by walking into the wind or seeking breezy places. Rather, the caribou stand facing downwind, their heads lowered almost to the ground, alert for the approach of the flies. They seem terrified by these pests, especially the nose bot. At the appearance of even one of the flies they shake their heads, stamp their feet and, if the attack continues, run wildly away. During late July and early August lone caribou or small groups may be seen racing over the tundra for no apparent reason; they are running from warbles or bot flies. Seeking refuge, caribou may also take to the water, wading or swimming to escape.

The time of recovery comes when the insect pests at last die off. In the cool, shortening days at summer's end the caribou must feed and feed more to replenish their strength for the travels of autumn, for the coming battles of the rut, and for the long dark days of winter, which come all too soon to the northern lands.

Pages 70-71: A post-calving herd masses on the green hills above Bathurst Inlet, Northwest Territories.

Pages 74-75: Ogilvie Mountains, Yukon.

Pages 76-77: A post-calving herd of several thousand animals pours over the hills above Bathurst Lake, Northwest Territories. Some post-calving herds contain thirty times this many caribou!

Page 78: Yellow-billed loons, Bathurst Lake, Northwest Territories.

Page 79 (from left to right): Alpine azalea; arctic ground squirrel, Wager Bay, Northwest Territories; mountain avens; flowers of tundra blueberry; a brooding ptarmigan in her summer camouflage plumage, Beaufort Lagoon, Alaska; newly hatched goslings in the downy nest of a Canada goose, Taltson River, Northwest Territories; woolly lousewort; cottongrass heads glow in the evening light near the Firth River, Yukon.

Page 80: Nestling peregrine falcons, Wager Bay, Northwest Territories.

Page 82: Bathurst herd at a water crossing near Contwoyto Lake, Northwest Territories.

Page 83: Bathurst herd at a water crossing near Contwoyto Lake, Northwest Territories.

Pages 84-85: Caribou at a traditional water crossing near Contwoyto Lake, Northwest Territories.

Page 86: Caribou pour onto a snow patch in an attempt to find relief from mosquitoes, near Bathurst Lake, Northwest Territories.

Pages 88-89: Calves learn by trial and error which plants to eat, but by grazing close to their mothers they have a much better chance of finding the most nutritious species. Beaufort Lagoon, Alaska.

Pages 90-91: A small band of young bulls gallops over the tundra, British Mountains, Yukon. Warble flies and nose bots often cause such panicked attempts by the caribou to escape.

Page 92 (upper): Haloed by the golden sun that never sets in the arctic summer, a band of caribou grazes in a cottongrass meadow.

Page 92 (lower): Caribou seek relief from heat and insects on the overflow ice of the Kongakut River, Alaska.

Page 93 (upper): A small fraction of the tens of thousands of caribou in the Bathurst herd grazes on the lush summer tundra near Bathurst Lake, Northwest Territories.

Page 93 (lower): Caribou trails lead to a traditional water crossing, Contwoyto Lake, Northwest Territories.

Page 94: The antler velvet is clearly visible on this bull, as are the patches where the old coat is being shed and the new coat is growing in. Near Point Lake, Northwest Territories.

Page 95: Calf killed by wolf along the migration trails of the Bathurst herd. The wolf has eaten only the brains, tongue, and a small part of the innards.

Page 96: Cows lead their calves across a stream connecting with Bathurst Lake, Northwest Territories.

Autumn
The hunter's moon

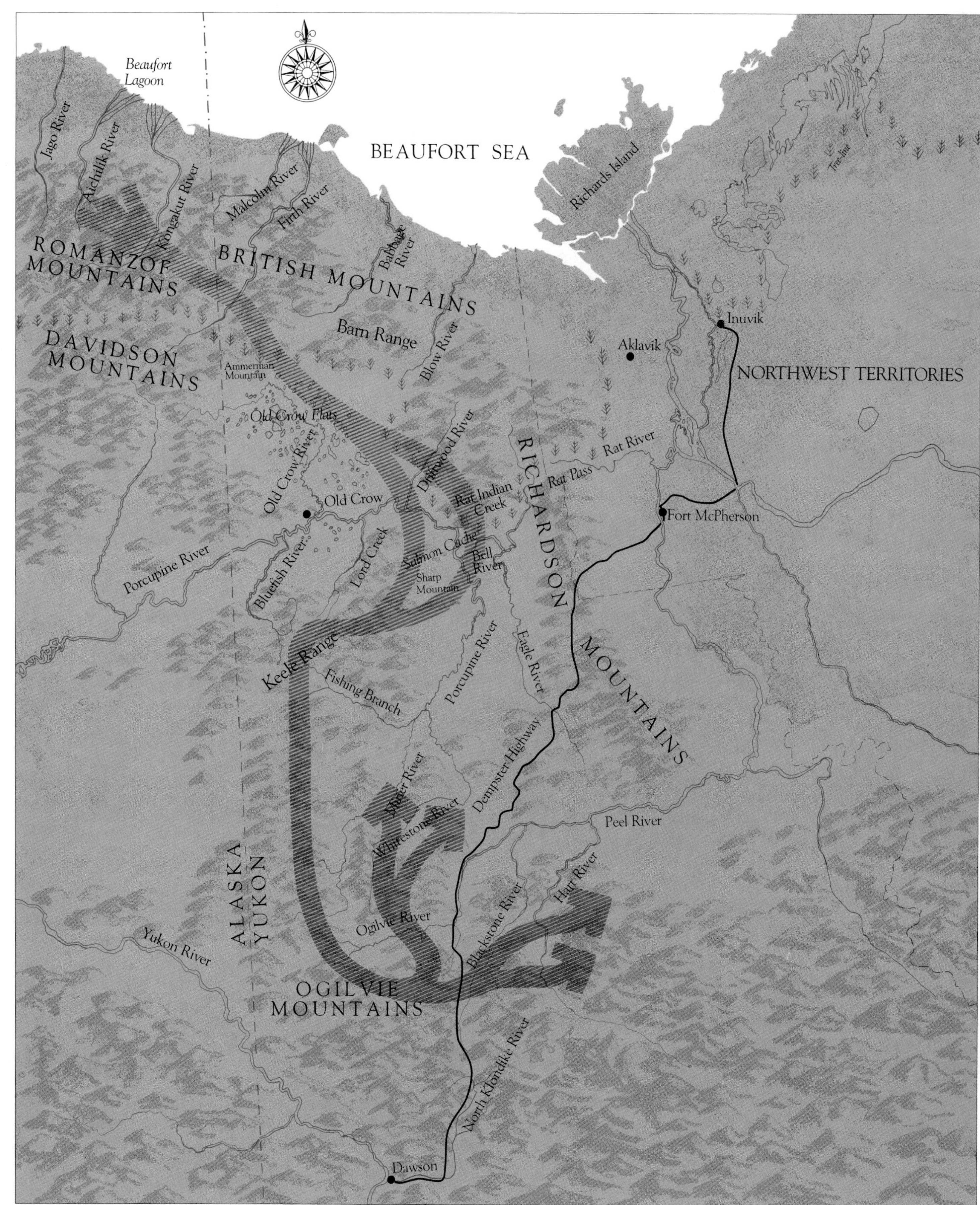

An autumn migration of the Porcupine herd

There is a time in the far North, between the heat and bugs of summer and the long dark winter, when all life seems good and easy. The days are still warm, the nights now crisp for sleeping. Blueberries and bright cranberries hang ripe on their bushes; frosts have painted the land in crimson, gold, and scarlet. Against the blue sky broods of wildfowl are on the wing, and the ptarmigan are flocking in the hills. The waters teem with the autumn runs of lake trout, whitefish, and arctic char. And the hunting peoples know that this best of all seasons will bring the greatest gift of the northern lands: the return of the caribou, heavy-furred and rich with fat.

The Porcupine River slid swiftly beneath the high bank on which the village of Old Crow sat perched. Small eddies and upwellings swirled the coffee-coloured surface; the silty water hissed against the boat nosed up on the pebbles of the beach. The hunter carried his last load down the steep path.

Word had come downriver that morning, the news he had been waiting for. As soon as he heard, the hunter started to get his outfit together. If he left Old Crow this afternoon, he could be there tomorrow morning. The caribou were crossing at Salmon Cache!

He rested for a moment, catching his breath as he looked along the beach. He could see the rack of drying salmon and smell the smoke from the willow smudge beneath the fish. The hunter breathed in the familiar smells of autumn. Somewhere back among the houses a pack of chained-up huskies started to howl. He began to load.

In the centre of the boat he put four ten-kegs of mixed gas for the motor. Then he packed the camp: his heavy sleeping robe and a rolled-up caribou hide for a mattress; a grey and spark-holed canvas wall tent; the battered travelling stove with its lengths of pipe inside; a small Hudson's Bay axe; the grub box with the matches, cooking gear, tea, sugar, flour, salt and pepper, and a few tins. Near his seat he placed the canvas hunting bag containing his skinning knives, five new boxes of .30-30 ammunition, and a pouch of .22 bullets. Against the bag he leaned the old Winchester, its barrel shiny with years of service, and the .22. Then he untied the boat. With a spruce pole he pushed the boat out into the current and pulled the starter on the twenty-horse kicker. The river surged against the bow. Three children stopped their play along the bank and watched the boat glide away.

The hunter passed the mouth of the Old Crow River where it empties into the Porcupine, swinging wide to avoid the bleach jug floats that marked the fish nets set there. He rounded the first bend; the village disappeared from sight. Leaning forward, he reached for his parka and put it on against the chill of the river.

As the boat droned upstream, the hunter watched the bends unfold one by one, each familiar to him from a lifetime of travelling the river. He passed the high banks of "Caribou Lookout," then between the big islands just above. He steered with unconscious ease, avoiding the shallow sand-bar off a point, then hugging the shore where the current was not so fast, crossing the channel in anticipation of an obstacle or an advantage ahead. A flock of golden-eyes came whistling down the river. They flared slightly when they saw the boat, flashing black and white. At each turn a new vista opened, sometimes high cutbanks, sometimes a stand of dark spruce, then a gravel beach and tall willows with a few yellow leaves still fluttering. The distant hills swung across the horizon as the hunter rounded the bends. A flight of swans winging down from the Old Crow Flats passed high overhead, a wavy white line against the sky.

Two and a half hours later the boat grated on the stones as the hunter pulled in at the mouth of Lord Creek. Driftwood lay in heaps at the high-water line; within minutes he had a fire blazing. He dipped the blackened tea billy into the stream and set it on the fire. While he waited for the water to boil, he got tea and sugar from the grub box, and a piece of dry meat. The hunter watched the ducks passing along the river: mostly mergansers and golden-eyes, but a few mallards and a flock of widgeons too. The warmth of the tea and the fire felt good. The tea stop over, he put his things away and pulled again on the starter cord.

When the hunter reached the riffles above Lord Creek, a movement on shore caught his eye. A porcupine was waddling along the bank at the edge of the willows. Its golden guard-hairs shone in the sun. The hunter immediately turned towards shore. When the bow touched, he hopped over the load, ran to a pile of driftwood where he picked up a heavy stick, and approached the hapless animal. With three swift blows he killed it. The hunter loved the porcupine's fat, resin-flavoured meat, and now he had his dinner. Quickly he built another fire and, putting on his leather mitts, he turned the porcupine over and over in the flames to singe off the quills and guard-hairs. Then he tossed the animal in the bow and set out upriver to make a few more miles before nightfall.

It was almost dark when the hunter pulled ashore. After tying up the boat, he carried the tent and stove to a grove of spruce. Tent poles were already there, cut on a previous trip. With an efficiency born of a lifetime's experience, he made camp. First he set up the tent, lashing the rear of the ridge pole to a spruce, and supporting the front with a pair of crossed poles. Then he pieced together the rusty lengths of stovepipe, poked the chimney through the hole in the canvas, and set it into the stove. He went to the boat for the axe and grub box. In the gathering dusk he cut a dead spruce into stove-lengths. As the fire crackled to life, he filled the billy and brought up his sleeping robe. While the water heated, he cut several armloads of spruce boughs and layered them opposite the stove. On top of these he spread the big caribou hide and placed his bedroll for a back rest. It was dark now. He lit a candle and stuck it on the top of a can. Shadows danced on the canvas. The hunter reclined on his bed with a cup of strong sweet tea, leaning comfortably against the bedroll. Heat filled the tent. He could smell the cut spruce boughs. He closed his eyes for a minute. . . .

After his meal of porcupine, bannock, and more tea, the hunter walked out into the night chill. He could see his breath against the stars. The moon began to rise over the hills, huge and yellow-orange. A hunter's moon. He smoked a cigarette, listening to the river sliding by and watching the moon rise. Then he went in and unrolled his sleeping bag.

He was back on the river at sunrise. In the early light the boat's wake gleamed against the flat dark water. On the bank, stones and tall willows sparkled with half-melted frost. There were tracks on the sand-bars near the mouth of the Driftwood River; some caribou were crossing here, but he continued upriver. Before the hunter reached Salmon Cache he could smell the smoke. Then he saw the fire and the boats pulled up on the shore and the other hunters standing by. Ribs were dangling from a forked stick by the fire. As he nosed the boat in, the others put on the tea billy.

The bulls lay panting in the sun. In the surprising warmth of the Indian summer afternoon they were uncomfortable. Their rapidly growing winter coats and the thickening layer of fat on their backs held in their body heat. Their tongues lolled out; they flicked their ears and blinked in

minor irritation at the few late blackflies buzzing around their faces. Seven of the bulls rested on their chests, legs drawn up under them, chewing their cuds. The eighth lay flat on his side, one of his big velvet-covered antlers sticking up like a dead branch.

The caribou were lying on the brushy slopes of Ammerman Mountain overlooking the Old Crow Flats. Now, at the end of the first week of September, the tundra colours flamed at their peak of brilliance. In August, when frost had started to come at night, the willows had changed first, outlining the stream margins with gold. A few more clear cold nights turned the bearberry leaves blood-red. Then the dwarf birches took on their glowing orange hue. All the colours of an autumn hardwood forest were there in miniature, though no plant stood taller than four feet. Blueberries, crow-berries, and cranberries hung on their bushes. A big flock of ptarmigan in mottled fall plumage flew across the hill from one patch of berries to another.

One of the bulls got up and began to feed. He was the largest, and his massive antlers were unusual in having two big brow tines instead of just one, as most males have. Hunters would call him a "double-shovel" bull, from an old belief that the bulls use their brow tines to shovel away the snow when feeding. He foraged for several minutes and then ambled over to a small sturdy spruce. He lowered his head, put the top points of his antlers against the tree, and rubbed them back and forth against the trunk. His efforts ripped bark and branches from the tree, and tears appeared in the velvet covering the antlers, blood showing brightly on the white bone underneath. His companions rose one by one and began to feed. The eight bulls moved down the hill, grazing and occasionally rubbing their antlers against the bushes. Their white manes glowed in the afternoon light.

The eight had been together since the big summer herd broke up at the end of July. They had first travelled west, across the north side of the Old Crow Flats, into the mountains around the headwaters of the Kongakut River. In these high valleys the bulls had fed heavily and had started to put on fat. Then in late August, when the frosts began to kill the plants in the mountains, they had moved down to the main rivers, drifting across the hills east of the Kongakut and into the Firth drainage. In the willow thickets along these rivers the caribou had encountered groups of bull moose. The huge dark moose had already begun cleaning their antlers on the willows. A few were beginning to call. Their rut was fast approaching.

The double-shovel bull and his group had travelled east

across the Firth to Ammerman Mountain. Now the eight bulls continued along the northern edge of the Flats. Although many bands of cows and immature animals were moving in the same direction, the bulls kept to themselves. Their antler-rubbing became more frequent. Velvet hung in long strips from the antlers of the double-shovel bull, and pieces dangled in the bushes where he rubbed. The other bulls too worked to rid themselves of the irritating tatters. Their bloody antlers vied with the bearberry for brilliance.

By the middle of September the double-shovel bull had completely shed his velvet. Dried blood and bark stains from the bushes had already darkened his antlers. The big bull was starting to spar with his companions. He would approach another bull and lower his head, placing the top points of the antlers forward and close to the ground. When the other male responded in the same way, they would mesh antlers and twist and shove, trying to push each other off balance. These contests were good-natured, involving little of the violence of the coming battles of the rut.

The tundra colours were quickly losing their brilliance. Every night there was frost. Leaves withered and turned brown. Blueberries puckered and dropped off the bushes. Many of the shallow ponds on the Flats were already frozen. When the strong steady wind from the northwest began in the afternoon of September the seventeenth, flock after flock of waterfowl took off, rose on rapid wings against the evening glow, and set a course to the south. The wind continued for several hours and then the blizzard struck. Fierce winds buffeted the country all night; by dawn six inches of heavy wet snow covered the Flats. The spruce and dwarf birch were plastered white. The blizzard left no doubt that Indian summer was over and seven months of hard winter were on the way.

With the first grey light the double-shovel bull got to his feet and started southeast across the Flats. Other caribou left the area too, moving off with a purposeful gait. Bands joined when they met; bulls now mingled with cows and their young ones. Snow fell all that day, veiling the lines of moving caribou, the white flakes sticking to their brown backs. By nightfall the eight bulls and the caribou that had joined them had covered twenty-six miles. They continued steadily all the next day. The caribou were now migrating in earnest, in contrast to the leisurely drift that had characterized their movements during the fine weather.

Most of the lakes were now frozen, but the ice was thin. On several ponds holes showed that a caribou had broken through, leaving behind a channel filled with chunks of ice where the animal had smashed its way back to shore. On one lake was a small hole in the ice that a pair of swans had kept open by constant swimming around. The birds had stayed with their flightless cygnet until the last possible moment, waiting for it to gain the final bit of growth that would put it on the wing. Now they were gone. A bald eagle sat on the ice, feeding on the remains of the cygnet for whom winter had come just a few days too soon.

As the snow began to melt, dripping off the bushes and becoming slushy underfoot, the caribou slowed a little. But they kept moving southeast until they reached the Driftwood River. The eight bulls now travelled in a group numbering around two hundred animals, including other large bulls, many younger males, and cows accompanied by calves and yearlings. Within the migration the big bulls remained in a group by themselves. The entire herd was now spread out over many miles. The vanguard animals were already crossing the Porcupine River. The eight bulls did not reach Salmon Cache until two days later.

The hunter sat in his boat on the south side of the Porcupine. He smoked a cigarette and watched the river. For over an hour nothing had crossed at his place, but tracks on the sand on both shores told him that caribou had crossed here yesterday. He could hear shooting from the other hunters downstream. When he saw the first cow step out of the willows across the river, he took the cigarette out of his mouth and tossed it into the current.

The cow came out a few feet and stopped. Her calf moved up behind. Then she turned and started along the shore, where patches of snow still lay among the smooth stones. Every few yards the cow halted and looked at the current and down the shore. More and more caribou emerged from the willows, following her in single file. As the hunter watched, the big double-shovel bull stepped onto the shore.

The caribou walked for a quarter of a mile, then stopped and stood still. Finally the cow moved hesitantly to the water and, after a final halt at the edge, waded in. One by one her companions followed, swimming in single file, their white tails held high. The line of swimmers undu-

lated in the current. Still the hunter did not move. He waited until the leader had crossed about a third of the distance before he started the motor. He intercepted the line of swimming caribou just before the cow got her footing on the bottom. Putting the motor in neutral, he reached for his rifle and started shooting as the lead animals splashed ashore around his boat. The hunter was after bulls only, for they were the largest and fattest. He killed four while they were still swimming. Then as the caribou began to splash through the shallows, he shot another one, missed once, and was out of ammunition. While the hunter hurriedly stuffed cartridges into his rifle, the double-shovel bull and his companions gained the shallows. As they crossed the beach the hunter killed one, then fired again as they disappeared into the trees. The bullet smashed the front leg of one of the bulls just above the ankle. He hobbled into the woods.

Many of the caribou had turned around and were now swimming back to the north side of the river. The hunter did not try to catch them, for they were almost ashore; nor did he try to find the animal that had limped off into the woods. He put the motor in gear and went after the dead bulls that were drifting downstream.

The hunter tied the floating carcasses alongside and towed them back to the beach. There he untied the four from the boat and pulled them onto shore near the last bull he had killed. He also retrieved the animal that had died in the shallows. With his kill all safely on shore, he cut some willows and laid them in the bottom of the boat. Then he began to butcher.

With each carcass he first cut off the head and placed it aside, resting on the antlers. Then he slit the skin down the length of the belly, but did not peel it away from the flanks. He did not intend to skin the caribou until he got back to Old Crow; that way the meat would stay clean during the trip. Then he opened the body cavity and removed the entrails. He carefully took out the edible organs — heart, liver, and kidneys — and placed them on the clean willows in the bottom of the boat. He also cut off the mesenteries, the membranes that hold together the coils of the intestines, for they were laced with fat. He stored these in a canvas bag. When all the animals were gutted, he chopped the antlers off the heads, and tossed the heads into the boat. They were special delicacies, rich with fat. His wife would boil them to make soup.

With these tasks done, the hunter took his rifle and walked into the bush where the last bull had disappeared. He searched for a moment or two, and found a few drops of blood. He tried to trace the blood trail, but soon lost it in the confusion of tracks where the caribou had raced away from the river. He followed the tracks for about a hundred yards but, seeing nothing more, he returned to the boat and made his way to camp. The other hunters had fat ribs roasting over the driftwood fire, and the tea pail was dangling from a forked stick.

Early the next morning the hunter killed four more caribou and quickly butchered them while his companions broke camp. Then they all left for home. The five Indians had killed sixty animals. Two of the hunters made a raft of their caribou by tying them on either side of a rectangular frame of spruce logs. The hollow hair of the caribou's coats kept the carcasses afloat, and in this way two boats could tow forty animals. The remainder were loaded into the other two boats. With the current now aiding him, the hunter arrived back in Old Crow late that afternoon. He left his kill in the boat until the next day, covering it with a tarp to discourage stray dogs and ravens.

Although it was freezing at night, the days were still warm and sunny. When the hunter cut up his meat, he hung the quarters in his smokehouse and built a small willow smudge. The fire kept flies away and gave the meat a slight crust to prevent it from spoiling before the deep-freezing weather arrived. His wife made many pounds of dry meat for use on the trail in winter, and also saved the flat strips of sinews from the loins for sewing moccasins. She cut the hair off several hides to prepare them for tanning. The hunter tacked up the rest on the logs of their cabin to dry for sleeping skins.

The river was now running ice. The pans glittered in the sun, tinkling as they slid by the village. More boats arrived from upstream, just ahead of freeze-up. The village hunters had now brought in over five hundred caribou. Everyone was secure with meat for another winter.

After their encounter with the hunter, the double-shovel bull and his group trotted through the spruce muskeg away from the river. They soon settled down, and after a mile or two were walking slowly and beginning to feed. They regrouped easily in the open woods, for they had not scattered far, and those that had strayed used their sense of smell to follow the trails left by others. The wounded bull tried to keep up with the herd, but soon fell

behind. He limped along in their path for a while and then lay down to rest.

The migration moved southwest through a range of low hills, across the headwaters of Johnson Creek and into the Keele Range. The double-shovel bull and his five remaining companions continued together, but the composition of their band kept changing as they merged with other groups, then broke apart again. The wounded bull hobbled along as best he could. His head bobbed deeply up and down as he shifted his weight from the broken front leg to the good one. His leg had become inflamed and painful, and he was weakening. Although he was unable to keep up with any travelling band, he nevertheless continued along the herd's trail.

A week later the wounded bull could barely rise. In the early morning he lay alone on a brushy slope near Sharp Mountain. A grizzly bear came padding and sniffing along the migration trail, looking for carrion or crippled caribou. Already he had found and eaten the carcass of a yearling that had been wounded at the river crossing, when one of the hunters had fired into a herd massed on the shore. The bear's heavy dark coat rippled with autumn fatness as he moved; the silver guard-hairs shone over his neck and hump. Catching the scent of the wounded bull, he crouched and started stalking upwind. When he saw the bull, the grizzly flattened closer to the ground and crept towards him with a stealth that belied his size and power. At twenty yards the bear charged. Few animals can cover a short distance faster than a grizzly. Although the caribou heard him coming and began scrambling to his feet, the bear slammed into him before he got his balance, and rode him to the ground. The bear's five-hundred-pound bulk held the caribou down while his powerful jaws clamped at the base of the skull. The bull was dead in seconds.

The bear fed fully and then covered the carcass with dirt, sticks, and leaves. He slept near the kill for several days, eating hugely whenever he felt like it. When he finally left, little remained; that was his last meal for the year. The grizzly wandered back to his den on a southeast-facing slope. He had already cleaned out this den, which he had used for his winter quarters for several years. Now he brought in grasses and other plants to make a nest for sleeping, and crawled inside.

As the caribou migrated south through the Keele Range, winter descended on the land with finality. Several inches of ice covered the ponds and streams. Now when storms swept through, the snow remained on the ground. Along the ridges snow buntings and horned larks sailed like leaves before the wind. Ground squirrels no longer bounded back to their burrows at the approach of the caribou; they already lay dormant underground. The forage plants had withered and frozen, and the caribou began to switch to their winter diet of lichens and dried sedges.

The big double-shovel bull now presented a magnificent picture of power and fitness. His neck was swollen to twice its normal size by the physiological changes of the coming rut. The long white mane and flank stripes contrasted vividly with his rich brown coat. His massive antlers, darkened and polished by a month of mock combat with small trees and bushes, gleamed as he walked along the ridges. The females were also in full autumn pelage, their colour patterns similar to the males but somewhat drabber, the manes and side stripes less showy.

By mid-October a terrible restlessness had seized the double-shovel bull. He had almost stopped feeding. His sparring became more violent; he now regarded all other bulls as adversaries. He surged through the herd with his swollen neck stretched out menacingly, uttering a hoarse rhythmic grunting. When he encountered other bulls, he trotted at them antlers down. Young bulls ran away, but some of the big bulls stayed to fight. These contests usually began with the double-shovel bull and his rival walking parallel to one another, grunting loudly, and tilting their heads to display their antlers. Then suddenly they would turn towards each other, smash the top points of their antlers into contact, and begin pushing and twisting, each trying to establish superiority by forcing the other back or throwing him off balance. The combatants whirled and slipped and skidded, their hooves tearing furrows in the snow and kicking up clumps of frozen turf.

Because of his size the double-shovel bull won these rutting battles. Usually the other bulls just disengaged and ran away after he drove them backwards. But one opponent was slow in moving off, and the big bull gored him in the side, breaking several ribs. The wounded animal staggered into the bush, where he died.

The big bull adopted the same low neck stretch in approaching the females. He walked alongside the cows, grunting, displaying his antlers, and occasionally curling back his lips and protruding his tongue. He sniffed the cows' genitalia for the first signs of oestrus. But the cows would not yet stand, and moved away. So the big bull

paced from cow to cow, threatening or fighting any animals that got in his way.

The migration had now reached the Ogilvie Mountains. Caribou bands were scattered over the brushy flats along the rivers and in the low open hills. In the treeless terrain the caribou could easily see each other; groups continually met and merged. Animals exchanged between bands, and now all ages and both sexes were mixed among the groups. When two bands met, there was a flurry of activity as the bulls challenged each other and tested the new cows for readiness. Sounds of clattering antlers and grunting bulls carried over the land. Herds seethed with constant turmoil as the bulls displayed, fought, and pursued the cows. Bewildered calves tagged behind their mothers while trying to stay out of the way of the heedless bulls. Cows tried to feed or rest and chew their cuds despite the harassment.

The turmoil increased in intensity until the third week of October, when the cows began to come into heat. Now the double-shovel bull found receptive cows, and he tended them. After approaching with the low neck stretch, the bull curled back his lip and made a loud slurping lick with his tongue. Sometimes he directed the licking at the cow's vulva, but he also did it while standing alongside her. If the cow failed to move off, the big bull stationed himself beside or behind her and waited. Often he stood in an awkward-looking position with his hind feet close together and drawn up under him. His back was arched and his head lowered, as he stared at the ground in front of him. The bull stood this way for minutes on end. Sometimes he urinated and trampled it into the ground; if the cow urinated, he smelled and licked the place. If she moved off, he followed in the low neck stretch position, grunting and lip-curling until she stopped and he could once again take up his waiting posture.

At last the big bull would try to mount. Often the cow shifted a few steps just as he lifted his front quarters off the ground, and he had to readjust his position; sometimes many such unsuccessful attempts preceded the final breeding. The actual copulation occurred remarkably quickly, in a matter of seconds. The bull rose up, covered the cow, gave a few quick thrusts, and slid off. Some of the females stumbled and fell under his weight. As soon as he had bred each cow, the big bull lost interest in her and quickly moved off to find another.

For one more frenzied week the great bulls fought each other and bred the cows. Then, as abruptly as the rutting had developed, it faded with the passing of oestrus among the females. The double-shovel bull was thin and exhausted. The stores of fat he had built up over July, August, and September had been almost completely dissipated in the two weeks of ceaseless battle and exertion.

Snow was falling in the forested valleys of the Ogilvie Mountains. The landscape took on the white and grey monochrome of winter. Days of biting cold arrived. Soon the Ogilvie winter range would be the coldest place in North America.

The double-shovel bull once again joined the other males. The antagonism of the rut was gone. Soon the largest bulls began to shed their antlers; most had done so by mid-November. The younger, smaller males, who had not been sexually active, retained theirs through most of the winter. The females no longer held any attraction for the males. Gradually they separated themselves from the company of cows and calves, a segregation that would last through the winter and spring. Together the big bulls moved into the snow-silenced forests to face another winter.

In many ways the caribou's migration in autumn mirrors their spring journey. It brings them back from the tundra to the forests where they will winter. As in spring, dispersed animals gradually group together and begin drifting along the migration route, quickening their pace as the season wears on. The autumn routes lead to particular winter ranges that are traditional and relatively predictable. But whereas spring migration is largely the story of the cows' journey to their calving grounds, in autumn the sexes must travel together. For the brief but violent rut occurs during the autumn migration, and the sexes must breed to perpetuate the species.

In August the caribou are widely scattered following the break-up of the great summer herds. Bands of more than a hundred animals are rarely seen. Big bulls graze by themselves, and the cows, calves, and young animals travel apart from the mature males. The disappearance of the insects that harass the caribou in summer releases them from the drain of constant travel and fitful feeding. They wander slowly, grazing peacefully, and begin to put on fat. They seek out the lushest, most nutritious vegetation. In Alaska and the Yukon many caribou spend the late summer and early autumn high in the mountains, feeding where lingering snowdrifts and cool temperatures have delayed the growth and flowering of plants. Caribou on the barrens select sedges and horsetails, which grow in wet habitats and thus remain green and nutritious longer than the vegetation on drier sites. In early September I have seen caribou from the Beverly herd wading out belly-deep in ponds, looking for all the world like moose as they fed on the dense growth of sedges. Caribou also search avidly for mushrooms, which sprout in the late summer and early fall. In some areas these fungi may constitute a major part of their diet. For example, in the rumen samples of caribou from interior Alaska in late August, fungi comprised forty-five per cent of the total food volume, and in one animal accounted for eighty-four per cent of the stomach contents.

When the first frosts of autumn begin to streak the tundra with colour, the caribou start a leisurely drift towards the tree-line. At first the movement to the winter ranges is slow and gradual, and bulls and cows remain in separate groups until well into September. As the frosts become heavier and the herbaceous vegetation withers, the caribou's diet becomes more restricted and they start to switch to the lichens and other plants that will be used during the winter. Despite the change, the animals continue to put on fat throughout September. This pattern of dramatic weight gain by males before the rut is common to most northern ungulates, including mountain sheep, musk-oxen, deer, moose, and wapiti. In none of these species, however, is the increase in weight and fat so great as in caribou.

A mature breeding bull increases in weight by twenty per cent or more between July and late September, a gain mostly accounted for by deposits of fat. In preparation for the exertions of the rut, a bull stores fifty pounds or more of rich white fat in solid layers up to three inches thick across the rump and lower back. Fat globules form on the mesenteries of the intestines, around the kidneys, and on the inside of the body cavity itself. Lesser amounts are deposited in the bone marrow, behind the eyes, and in other places in the head and neck.

The females too put on weight in autumn, but their gains are much less dramatic, averaging slightly over ten per cent of their body weight. The rump fat of females is generally little over half an inch deep, and the internal fat deposits are proportionately less. The bulls reach their peak of weight and condition just before the rut, and then expend almost all of their stored energy in a short frenzy of reproductive effort. The females lose little or no weight in breeding, and put on fat well into November.

While the physical condition of the caribou is improving, so too is their appearance. The shedding of old hair, which gives the caribou's summer coat a patchy, moth-eaten look, is usually complete by mid-August. The newly moulted animals are dark brown, with a short smooth coat. The guard-hairs grow out rapidly. Within a month the bulls have heavy white manes and white stripes along their flanks, contrasting vividly with the dark coats; females do not produce such substantial manes and stripes. By autumn the holes in the hides produced by the emergence of warble fly larvae in June have healed with scar tissue.

The bulls begin to rub the velvet off their antlers in late August or early September. By this time the antlers are fully grown and hard under the velvet, and the extensive blood circulation of the growing period has been greatly reduced. The bulls rub and work the antlers back and forth against small trees and clumps of brush to peel off the skin. They rub so vigorously that bark and branches are broken off the trees. Along traditional migration routes "rubbing trees" are common: small spruce, larch, and pines that have been killed or misshapen by the bulls. The process of shedding takes several days, and at first the white antlers may be covered in blood from the residual circulation beneath the velvet. A big bull caribou moving through the brilliance of the autumn tundra, his antlers blood red against the blue September sky, is a sight never to be forgotten. The younger bulls shed several days later than the adults, and the cows are not completely free of velvet until shortly before the rut.

Because the caribou are in prime condition, autumn is the time of the hunt for native peoples. It is the only period of the year when the caribou carry large quantities of fat, and hides free of warble fly holes. An additional advantage of an autumn hunt is that the weather is cold, and large quantities of meat can be preserved by freezing. For millennia the hunting peoples of the northern hemisphere have travelled to traditional locations along the autumn routes to intercept the caribou and kill enough for their winter food supply.

The first heavy snowfall of the year starts the rapid autumn migration. Prior to that first storm the caribou drift slowly and randomly, not always in the direction of the final fall routes. Once underway, the caribou migrate purposefully at speeds comparable to those in the spring: up to twenty miles a day. If storms come late, the migration is delayed; the dates of autumn migration vary as much as do those in spring. In some years large groups of caribou from herds that normally migrate to the forests

remain on the tundra throughout the winter. Perhaps in such cases the first blizzards come so late that the caribou have lost their physiological predisposition to migrate by the time the snow finally arrives.

Snow on the ground plays a less important role in autumn than it does in spring, for it rarely reaches sufficient depth to impede the animals. Weather and snowfalls may, however, determine which winter ranges the caribou use. I saw a striking instance of the effects of weather during two autumn migrations of the Porcupine herd. In early September 1971 a two-day blizzard drove the caribou out of the mountains on the Alaska-Yukon border and sent thousands of animals filing rapidly south across the Porcupine River, into the Keele Range. A spell of warm sunny days followed. The migration slowed and stopped. Then the herd turned around and headed north, back towards the river. By the end of September they had once again moved within sight of the river. I felt sure, as did the people of Old Crow, that they would recross the Porcupine. But on the last day of September a fierce blizzard drove them south once more, and in less than two weeks the herd was well within the winter ranges in the Ogilvie Mountains, 150 miles to the south. The following year the caribou followed a similar pattern, except that this time no storms came as they swung north towards the Porcupine River again. They recrossed the river and moved northwest into Alaska, where they spent the winter around Arctic Village and the east fork of the Chandalar River, some 300 miles from their previous wintering area in the central Yukon.

Usually the autumn migration is underway before the first sign of the impending rut: the bulls antler-sparring with one another after shedding their velvet. Initially these matches involve only minor clashes, with little serious shoving or contests of strength.

As the season progresses, physiological changes alter the appearance and behaviour of the mature bulls. Their necks swell to twice the normal size. They almost completely stop eating. Their livers degenerate, becoming yellow and mushy as the glycogen stores are depleted and ketone bodies accumulate. The big bulls begin to stink, perhaps as a result of glandular activity and altered metabolism. At this time of the year their meat is rank and inedible, and as a result hunters try not to kill bulls during the rut or for a month or more afterwards. An aggressive intolerance develops among the males. Their battles grow progressively more violent until at last, at the peak of the rut, they become terrible contests for dominance in which the big bulls may maim or even kill one another.

Among barren-ground caribou, rutting groups are large, most numbering more than a hundred animals. Since the rut takes place on the move, groups continually merge, break up, and exchange members. The herds travel through open country at this season, through large brushy openings in the boreal forest in Alaska and the Yukon, or on frozen lakes in central Canada. Since animals can see each other for long distances, there is a greater likelihood of groups coming together. Under these conditions the big bulls cannot form harems, as do some other deer such as wapiti or red deer. Bulls do not try to herd cows to keep them from straying; cows join and leave the herds freely. By contrast, in smaller, less mobile populations of woodland caribou, one bull may dominate a group, challenging, threatening, and fighting any other large male that approaches. In the rutting companies of barren-ground caribou, one male cannot dominate all the others; rather, many big bulls spend their time pursuing the cows and testing them for signs of oestrus. Fights usually break out when more than one pursues the same female.

The bulls use a stereotyped behaviour when courting the females. They advance with necks stretched forward, noses parallel to the ground, uttering a hoarse coughing sound, which has been variously termed "grunting," "snorting," "roaring," "rattling," and "panting." The bulls most often approach from behind, and try to sniff the cows' genitalia.

The bull's approach is a modified threat posture; the cow's reaction to it serves to inform him of her reproductive state. During the early stages of the rut when the female is not yet physically or psychologically prepared to mate, she interprets his behaviour as a threat and moves off. The bull may follow or chase the cow briefly, but he soon turns his attention to other females. Often as one bull follows a cow, another bull will join the chase, paralleling the first and displaying in the same way. During such encounters the bulls turn their heads to display their antlers prominently. Usually these confrontations result in the bulls simultaneously turning towards each other, locking antlers, and fighting. The sight and sound of their battle attract other males who rush to the scene and either pursue the cow that was the original object of the chase, or challenge the combatants themselves. Multiple fights often break out.

Battles between bulls are generally brief, lasting less than a minute. They frequently appear to end by mutual agreement of both opponents. If one bull gets pushed backwards, he may pull away and run off, averting his head and antlers, although his rival may chase him. Most fights result in little obvious harm to the bulls, but injuries do occur. Near the end of the rut I have seen caribou with broken antlers, large bleeding cuts, and bad limps. I also came across two combatants with antlers locked together. After half an hour of frantic fighting, they suddenly broke free and trotted away, but sometimes such predicaments end in a slow agonizing death for the trapped animals.

As the females begin to come into heat, they no longer run from the bulls. When a male finds a receptive cow he begins to tend her, following her everywhere and standing close by when she stops. The bull's common posture while tending is to wait motionless with head lowered almost to the ground, as though staring at a bush or clump of vegetation. This stance has been quaintly referred to as "bush-gazing," although it occurs just the same on the bare surface of frozen lakes, and its function has not been explained. While standing, the bull often urinates on his hind legs and tramples the urine into the ground. This behaviour, termed "hock-rubbing," probably constitutes both a visual and an olfactory stimulus to sexual activity in the female, and it may help carry odours from a gland between the toes. The smell of the cow's urine likely plays a part in conveying her readiness to the bull.

Copulation is so brief that it is difficult to imagine that the process could be shortened any more and still result in successful fertilization. The weight of a large bull often causes the females to stumble or fall; indeed, the upper limit to the size of male caribou may be set by the ability of the females to accommodate their weight during breeding. Unlike some other ungulates such as mountain sheep, in which the male repeatedly mounts a single female, multiple mountings do not occur in caribou. The male immediately loses interest in a cow once he has bred her, and moves on to locate and tend another oestrous female.

Most of the breeding takes place during a week or less, which accounts for the synchronized births of calves the following spring. The gestation period in caribou is between 227 and 229 days. Thus, for the herds in interior Alaska that calve in mid-May, the peak of the breeding season occurs during the first week in October. For the more northerly populations in arctic Alaska and Canada, the peak of the rut is two to three weeks later and may extend until the end of October. The height of the breeding season varies by several days from year to year, probably depending on weather and day length, which in turn is determined by the latitude.

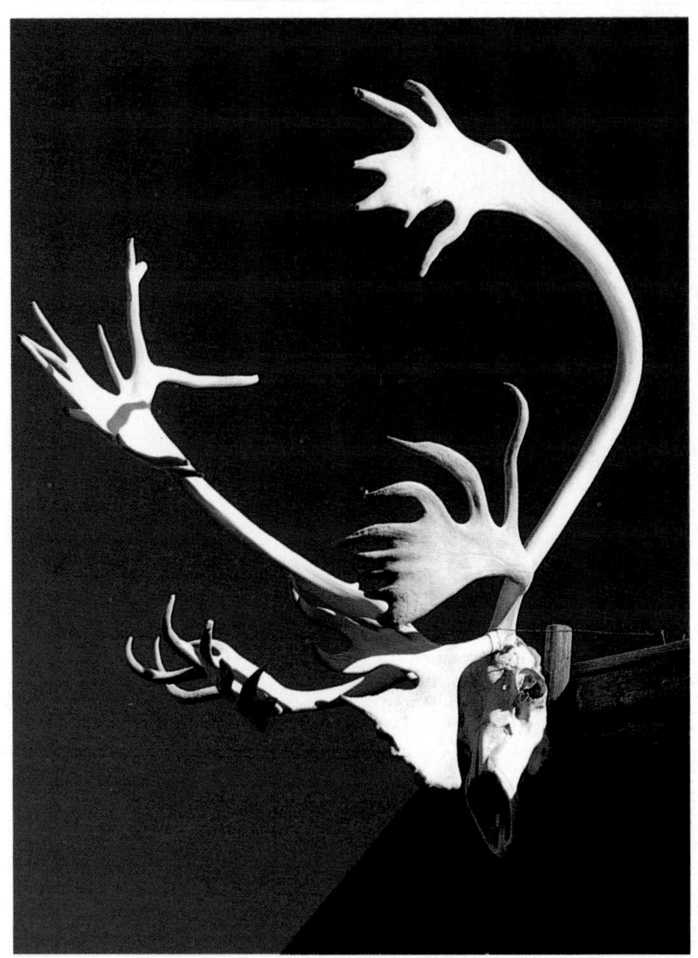

The largest bulls do most of the breeding. Since caribou bulls continue to grow in weight and antler development until six years of age, most of the sexually active animals are between five and ten years old. At the end of the rut, when the large males are exhausted and some have even begun to shed their antlers, younger bulls will breed the remaining unfertilized cows. Very old males become senile, and their antlers regress in size. Generally these animals remain on the periphery of the herds, avoiding the competition of the rut. The mortality rate of bulls is so high, however, that few live beyond ten years.

In almost all caribou herds there are more females than males: a ratio of two or more to one. Since the sex ratio at birth favours males slightly, they obviously have a higher mortality rate than females. Several factors contribute to the greater death rate of bulls. One is hunting, especially sport hunting. Hunters in the fall seek bulls because they are both larger and fatter than the cows; moreover, sport hunters look for bulls with the largest antlers for trophies. A correlation therefore exists between the intensity of sport hunting and the sex ratio in a caribou herd; the heavier the sport hunting, the lower the percentage of mature bulls.

But hunting alone cannot explain the greater mortality in males. The biology of the species and the environmental conditions under which the caribou have evolved also dictate that males will have a shorter life span than females. Among the adults of the herd, males generally account for thirty to forty per cent of the animals. Of these, less than one-third are breeding bulls in the five- to ten-year-old category. Thus each dominant bull must fertilize an average of about ten cows, and competition among these prime males is intense. Not only are the combatants injured and even killed during the rutting battles, but the rut simply exhausts the big bulls; they enter the winter drained of energy. Both direct injuries and their poor condition leave the bulls more vulnerable than the cows to the stresses of winter.

It appears unadaptive for the largest, most vigorous males to go into the long, brutally cold winters of the Arctic and Sub-arctic with their stores of fat depleted. But this may be the penalty that their ice-age history and adaptation to the North have imposed on the caribou. The northern climate allows only a short but highly productive growing season, followed by a long cold winter during which food is scarce. These conditions have strongly influenced the evolution of northern ungulates. Grazing animals have developed a short and precisely timed season of reproduction, so that the young are born just prior to the burst of plant growth in summer. With ample food during the summer, the males can store large quantities of fat and easily accumulate sufficient nutrients for the growth of enormous antlers. Stored fat frees the males from the need to feed during the intense battles and courtship displays of the rutting period. Those males that are the best fighters succeed in breeding the most females under these highly competitive conditions. Thus, among the bulls natural selection favours rapid growth, large body size, and massive antlers. Sexual maturation is delayed until these have been achieved.

The ultimate explanation of the higher mortality rate of bulls may simply be that males age more quickly. That is, in males natural selection favours those characteristics contributing to combat ability and high reproduction in a few seasons, at the expense of those conferring longevity. Conversely, females have only one offspring each breeding season; they are selected for early maturation and a long reproductive life. The short, violent, and exhausting rut of the caribou epitomizes the type of reproductive behaviour evolved by ungulates under arctic and sub-arctic conditions during the ice age. True, the battles and exertions of the dominant bulls and the characteristics for which they are selected may result in a shorter life expectancy, but success in evolutionary terms is measured not by longevity or individual survival, but by reproductive success.

How long a bull lives is of far less consequence than the number of calves he leaves behind during his few brief seasons of intense reproductive activity. The great bulls head into the harsh winter in poor condition, their fat reserves almost non-existent, but the needs of the species have been served. The embryos growing within the cows have been sired by the largest, most powerful, and aggressive of the herd's bulls.

AUTUMN PHOTOGRAPHS

Pages 98-99: Bulls on autumn tundra near Big Lake, Northwest Territories. During early September the mature bulls travel together in small groups away from the cows and young animals.

Page 102: Tundra colours near Big Lake, Northwest Territories.

Page 103: Kaleidoscope of colours produced by the leaves of dwarf birch, bearberry, willow, blueberry, and low-bush cranberry, Grizzle Bear Lake, Northwest Territories.

Pages 104-105: A hunter's moon, Porcupine River, Yukon.

Page 106: Hunter travelling by boat on the Porcupine River, Yukon.

Page 107: Hunters' camp on the Little Bell River, Yukon.

Pages 108-109: Tatters of velvet hang from the antlers of one of these bulls grazing near Providence Lake, Northwest Territories.

Page 111: Bull chasing a cow through the water, Blackstone River, Yukon.

Pages 112-113: Caribou swimming the Porcupine River during the autumn migration.

Page 114: Charlie Thomas skins a caribou on the bank of the Porcupine River, Yukon.

Pages 116-117: A grizzly bear and one of her cubs gobble up blueberries, Sable Pass, Alaska.

Page 117 (upper): Bull moose in early September blizzard, Savage River, Alaska.

Page 117 (lower): An arctic ground squirrel carries grass to make a nest in its winter hibernation burrow, Wager Bay, Northwest Territories.

Page 118: The antlers of this bull are stained with blood after the velvet has been rubbed off, Providence Lake, Northwest Territories.

Page 119: A big bull browses on willow and dwarf birch, Providence Lake, Northwest Territories.

Pages 121-123: Two big bulls battle during the rut, Ogilvie Mountains, Yukon.

Page 124: Two bulls chase a group of cows during the rut, Ogilvie Mountains, Yukon.

Page 125: A bull tends an oestrous cow, Ogilvie Mountains, Yukon.

Pages 126-127: A group of bulls and cows, near Contwoyto Lake, Northwest Territories.

Page 129 (upper): Bull tending a cow, Ogilvie Mountains, Yukon.

Page 129 (lower): Ellen Bruce of Old Crow places a caribou hide on a framework of willows for smoke-tanning.

Page 130: Caribou antlers on a cabin, Old Crow, Yukon.

Winter
The time of testing

Winter movements of the Beverly herd

Dark stretches of open water rippled beyond the shorefast ice, steaming in the cold. Although it was early November and well below zero, the vast volume of Selwyn Lake still had not frozen over. So this wide barrier of water, sprawling athwart the boundary of Saskatchewan and the Northwest Territories, confronted the hundreds of migrating bands of the Beverly caribou herd. The open lake split the migration. Most of the band moved south along the eastern shore, but many turned west, travelling between Selwyn and Ingalls lakes.

In one of the long files moving south a dark-faced calf trailed behind her mother through the falling snow. They had been steadily on the move since the first autumn blizzard near Dubawnt Lake had sent them hurrying out of the barren-lands. In a month they had covered over two hundred and fifty miles. But now the urge to travel was dying. The herd was well within the tree-line, into the lake-studded spruce forest of the Canadian Shield where they would spend the winter. The frenzy of the rut had faded away more than a week ago. The big bulls no longer surged through the herd, threatening and stirring up the other animals. Now drained and weak, the monarchs of the herd plodded along among the cows and calves. The largest males had already shed their antlers; they looked awkward and emasculated among their antlered companions.

At mid-morning the band emerged from the forest onto a frozen stream. The travelling file halted, then fell apart as the caribou scattered to feed on the abundant horsetails and water sedges along the banks. The soft snow yielded easily as the caribou snuffed in it with their broad muzzles and pawed to reach the still-green bases of the plants. Broken horsetail stems made dark patterns around the feeding craters. The dark-faced calf and her mother poked along the shore for half a mile as they fed.

With their bellies full, cow and calf moved to the middle of the stream and lay down. The calf regurgitated a mouthful of food and ground it methodically between her molars with an exaggerated sideways chewing. In a few minutes she swallowed and brought up another cud. After ruminating for an hour, the calf stood up and pawed a few times in the snow, then curled up in the crude bed and dozed. The light snow settled on her fur without melting. By noon the entire herd was lying down in scattered groups along the stream.

The caribou rested much of the afternoon before moving to the stream edge to graze again. A flock of willow ptarmigan was feeding in the bushes there. Curved black beaks snapped off bud after bud as the white birds fluttered among the branches, hurrying to fill their crops before plunging beneath the soft snow for the night. Among the willows crouched a snowshoe hare, motionless except for its rapidly moving jaws, stripping bark from the shrubs. Like the ptarmigan, the rabbit had turned white for the season of snow and was all but invisible in the shadows. Tracks criss-crossed the snow beneath the bushes: the precisely dotted trails of ptarmigan; the hop marks of hares, rear "snowshoes" ahead of the front feet; and one line of round, blurry prints left by the paws of a hunting lynx, the hare's deadliest predator.

The band left the stream just before dark and snaked through the tangled woods before trotting out onto a small lake. There they spent the night, lying together in one group several hundred yards from shore.

Even before the first light appeared in the southeastern sky, the dark-faced calf and her mother moved into the spruce to feed. Among the trees the cow started poking her nose into the snow, leaving marks on either side of the path she was breaking. She quickly smelled food and began pawing to reach it. The calf moved around her and began searching in the same way; soon she too was digging. Their broad hooves scooped back showers of loose snow. The cow uncovered a mat of lichen, stuck her head into the crater, and nibbled off the top inch or two of growth. Then she advanced into the unbroken snow, searching for more.

The pair returned to the lake soon after sunrise and bedded down to chew their cuds; their companions reappeared in ones and twos to join them. By mid-morning the entire band was bedded down again.

As the caribou lay on the snow, two wolves emerged from behind a spruce-covered island and strolled across the lake towards them. They got within a quarter of a mile before one cow spotted them. Abruptly her jaw stopped working on her cud and she raised her head high to stare at the figures moving against the snow. Nearby caribou, seeing her alertness, began searching for the object of her interest. The predators were not approaching directly, but quartering past the band, apparently paying them little attention. Still staring at the wolves, the first cow stood up slowly, thrust one hind leg to the side, and urinated, assuming the characteristic alarm posture.

Several nearby animals also rose and stood at alert, but most of the group remained lying down since the wolves had still displayed no sign of menace. As the wolves

continued away, obviously not hunting, five yearlings trotted after them. The curious youngsters paced in a tight group, heads held high, white tails standing straight up. Circling downwind behind the wolves to catch their scent, the yearlings suddenly pulled up. As the breeze carried the dread smell to their nostrils, they reared high on their hind legs, made a half turn in the air, and raced back to the security of the herd. Powdery snow showered up behind them.

The yearlings' excited leaps and galloping return stirred up the band; many more animals got to their feet. A couple of cows lowered their antlers in threat, moving a neighbour aside. Two young bulls locked antlers and sparred briefly. One calf tried to nurse, practically lifting its mother off her feet with a powerful bunt to the udder. The cow jumped and quickly stepped away. Animals milled around and then began to paw out new beds. But these small nervous actions soon ceased. The wolves were not long out of sight before the caribou, one by one, bent their forelegs and dropped back onto the snow.

It was snowing again as the band moved off in the afternoon. The caribou fed as they travelled through the woods towards another lake four miles to the southeast. The dark-faced calf pawed the snow beside her mother in the half-light of the evening forest. The animals were settling into the dull and repetitious routine of winter: feed, ruminate, rest, then feed again, always on the look-out for the hunting packs. Six more months of winter lay ahead. Six months of ploughing through snow, six months of cold and wind and meagre food that would drain their bodies and tax their every adaptation to the harsh northern world. The calf reached forward for the mouthful of lichens in the bottom of her crater.

It was a scene from another world. The ghostly northern lights shimmered and flowed across the sky, silhouetting the skeletal spruce. Against the dark trees the snow-covered lake gleamed brightly, but it was an eerie light, without shadows. Not a breeze stirred the bitterly cold air. Silence. Then a shudder and booming filled the night as vast forces of contraction sent cracks shooting for hundreds of yards across the three-foot-thick ice. The immense forces of space and cold played around the caribou as they lay curled on the ice of Phelps Lake.

At last the long night gave way to a rosy glow in the

southern sky. At the forest edge a flock of chickadees darted from tree to tree, foraging on small insects and pupae hidden in crevices in the bark. Their high thin notes carried far in the intense cold as the birds chattered back and forth. The dark-faced calf and her band stirred and rose. In a ragged file they headed for the spruce where the chickadees called.

The big island-littered expanse of Phelps Lake was the centre of the winter range for the eastern concentration of the Beverly caribou. On the surrounding lakes thousands of cows and calves in countless small bands were heading into the forest for their morning feed. The caribou had begun to arrive here in December, after working their way south through the numerous lakes and streams of the Porcupine River drainage. As the snow deepened, the caribou's rate of travel had slowed almost to a halt. Now, with January's bitter cold and darkness set in, the simple search for food demanded all their energy.

The bands around Phelps Lake consisted mainly of cows, calves, and yearlings, and many two- and three-year-old bulls. The big bulls had travelled far to the southwest into the jackpine country; they had begun their withdrawal soon after shedding their antlers in November, and had gradually drifted further and further from the female bands as winter wore on. The cows and juveniles would not see them again until the entire herd came together on the tundra in early July.

When the band reached the woods, deep blue shadows lay in the old feeding craters and the network of trails that they had made while foraging during days past. The trampled and dug-up snow had hardened, so the caribou sought undisturbed places that offered easier digging. The dark-faced calf and her companions followed an old trail across the trampled area, then broke a new path through to a ridge top half a mile from the lake. The past several days of windless cold had left a dusting of frost on the trees, and the low sun lit up the crystals like stained glass. Flakes sparkled silently to the ground as the caribou brushed the lower branches.

The spruce on the ridge stood far enough apart that an earlier wind had swept away some of the snow, leaving a shallower cover than in the dense woods below. The dark-faced calf followed her mother until the cow chose a feeding spot, then began her own searching nearby. They pawed mostly at the bases of the spruce, and were rewarded with lush mats of Cladina lichens and the waxy green leaves of low-bush cranberry.

Lichens and evergreen shrubs now formed the bulk of the caribou's food. The stands of sedges and horsetails they had fed on earlier in the winter now lay under drifts at the margins of lakes and streams. On this protein-poor diet of lichens, the caribou were slipping from their prime autumn condition. Already the cows had lost some weight and fat. But the biggest drain was yet to come, as winter wore on and on, snow piled deeper yet, and the demands of growing foetuses increased.

The sharp clattering of antlers now and then interrupted the muffled sounds of the feeding band, as two cows skirmished for possession of a crater. Once an antlerless cow walked over and threatened the dark-faced calf. When the smaller animal failed to give up her crater, the intruding cow laid back her ears and reared to strike with her hooves. As the calf shied away, her mother saw the attack. Plunging through the snow, she drove off the aggressor with lowered antlers.

Before noon the caribou trailed back to the lake and rested there, chewing their cuds in the bright but warmthless sun. Although the temperature hovered near forty below, their thick grey-brown coats insulated them completely as they lay on the snow, eyes half closed against the glare. The wolf packs hunting Phelps Lake had made many kills; the dark stains stood out sharply against the frozen lake. Loud croaks of ravens carried clearly as they squabbled over the scraps; otherwise the day was soundless. When the sun set in mid-afternoon, the caribou returned to the ridge, and it was long after dark before they filed back onto the lake. Many of the animals visited the forest for food once more in the middle of the night.

Next morning, as the dark-faced calf and her band headed into the woods to feed, they followed a snowmobile trail used by the resident trapper in making his rounds. The machine had packed the snow hard, offering invitingly easy walking for the caribou. They were perhaps a quarter of a mile into the trees when the lead animal suddenly stopped, splaying her hind legs in the alarm posture: she had heard a noise on the trail ahead. The caribou waited. The strange sound alone was not enough to send them fleeing until they had actually seen or smelled danger. Then, as the trapper came into sight astride his mechanical dog team, the caribou reared on their hind legs and scattered among the trees. The calf plunged through the soft snow behind her mother until they reached a packed caribou trail. They sprinted along this corridor of hard snow towards the safety of the lake.

As the cow and her calf lunged through the drifts along

the shore and onto the wind-packed lake, their companions were floundering out of the forest in several other places. The caribou ran together as soon as they saw one another, then bunched up and trotted further from shore. A couple of hundred yards out they stopped and faced back towards the forest. With heads alertly high, legs spread, and tails up, they waited. Breath steamed rhythmically from the nostrils of the panting animals and condensed in silver clouds above their heads.

When the noisy machine emerged from the screen of trees and stopped, the caribou watched motionless for several seconds, then in unison broke into a trot, circling the trapper. His cache was already full of frozen caribou, but he could not resist the temptation to shoot fresh meat. He got his rifle out. The lead animals halted and regarded the intruder, as they stood in the alarm position again. The trapper fired into the group and a cow fell kicking onto the snow. The dying animal's thrashing alarmed the rest and they moved away, milling indecisively. The trapper fired again with no obvious effect, then again. With renewed agitation the band reversed its direction and pranced past the other way. The trapper could see one animal hopping along on three legs. He fired at it several times before finally bringing it down.

Once more the caribou stopped, confused by the predator that did not pursue them. Suddenly they bolted and galloped back past the trapper, mouths open, straining for every bit of speed, kicking broken slabs of snow high into the air in their flight. He watched as the caribou streamed by, slowed, and continued on down the lake, the curious yearlings and young bulls halting now and again for a backward glance. Earlier in the season when he had no meat, he had relentlessly pursued bands such as this, firing again and again into the packed animals that refused to leave what they regarded as the safety of the open lake. The woodsman shook his head at the apparent stupidity of the caribou that made it so easy for him to get his meat. Then he jumped on his machine and went to retrieve his kill.

The caribou plodded along, their laboured breathing slowly returning to normal. Soon they headed into the woods to resume the all-important search for food.

The clack and clatter of colliding antlers echoed off the dark wall of spruce surrounding a little lake. Two young bulls were sparring playfully near the band of caribou resting on the ice. They had been at it steadily for more than half an hour; over and over they placed their spindly antlers together and shoved and twisted until one animal gave ground and trotted a few steps away. Sometimes one would sport about in a circle, bucking, kicking up his heels, even whirling around a couple of times before returning for another match.

The rapidly lengthening days of mid-March had generated an exuberance among the young males, urging them to combat and general playfulness. The cows resting nearby also felt the stirrings of spring, although their restlessness expressed itself not so much in play as in the urge to travel. In some mysterious way the long shadows cast by the late afternoon sun told the cows that the time had come to strike out for their calving grounds lying hundreds of miles to the north, still locked in ice and snow.

The weather, however, was not co-operating. A warm sunny spell had partially melted the snow a few days ago. The thaw and subsequent settling had started the cows drifting north. Then cold returned. Now the snow had crusted heavily, hindering both feeding and travel. The migration had halted.

At last the young bulls tired of their cavorting and headed into the woods to feed. The cows and young came soon after, the dark-faced calf still following her mother. In some places the crust supported the caribou, but mostly they broke through and floundered in the granular snow beneath. The going was so tough that the band went into the woods only a short way. The cow and her calf did not even attempt to dig in the hard snow, but rather began picking off the black hair-like tufts of tree lichens hanging from the spruce branches. Their sensitive lips carefully selected the lichens, breaking only the finest twigs. The cow also browsed on small branches and buds of willows. Her jaws, unsuited to woody foods, left the twigs frayed and chewed instead of neatly nipped off as a moose or mule deer would have done. Such food was more difficult to obtain in quantity than the ground lichens that had sustained the caribou since mid-winter; but it took less energy to get than anything under the snow.

For the next week and a half the caribou spent most of their time resting on lakes; the effort required to fight the snow in the forest was scarcely worth the forage gleaned from the trees. Some of the young bulls were now shedding their antlers. The cows chewed on the cast-off

antlers, trying to regain some of the minerals depleted over the long season of poor nutrition.

Then at last the weather warmed once more. As soon as the crusts softened, the cows lost no time getting underway again. In the sunny afternoons flocks of ravens played in the wind. Their strange liquid calls floated down from the clear sky as they wheeled and soared, pairing up for the approaching nesting. The big black birds had no shortage of food; remains of wolf kills lay scattered all over the winter ranges. Almost half the calves that had trailed behind their mothers in November had fallen to the packs over the winter. The wolves were fat, but it was otherwise with the caribou. The late spring crust coming on the heels of the deep snow of winter had pushed their reserves to a low ebb.

Fortunately this warm spell lasted. Heat waves swam over the lakes. Flocks of snow buntings arrived on the soft south wind. Red squirrels chattered from the spruce tops. Pairs of whisky-jacks whistled back and forth as they carried nest material to their secret places. Bare patches appeared around the dark tree trunks and on the southern exposures of eskers. The cows and their calves flocked to these oases that offered much needed food, free from the burden of digging.

Competition for the best feeding spots now took on a heightened seriousness. The rattle of antlers sounded regularly throughout the herd as the cows clashed over the right to feed in the open ground. The dark-faced calf stuck close to her mother. The cow fought off aggressors and let the calf feed beside her. Released at last from fighting snow for every mouthful, the caribou gradually regained some strength.

The time of testing was almost over. Already the small wintering bands were coming together into the long lines of spring migration. The cow was once again setting out on the northward journey that she had taken the year before, heading for the distant calving grounds where her dark-faced calf had been born. The season of renewal was at hand. Soon they would be on their way, out of the forests onto the windswept vastness of the barren-lands, to launch another generation into the endless cycle of the seasons.

In the temperate regions winter is a season; in the land of the caribou it is a way of life. Snow covers the land for eight months or more each year, from October to June. Everywhere they travel and in everything they do, the caribou must contend with this omnipresent blanket of the northern land. They may be conceived in the snow, born in the snow, and die in the snow. Temperatures plummet to −40°F and −50°F for days, even weeks, on end. Of all the world's species of deer, only the caribou have evolved to inhabit the Arctic. Thousands of years of survival in the northern lands have left these animals so highly adapted to life under winter conditions that they have been termed "chionophiles," or snow-loving animals.

The relentless cold of the northern ranges, which seems such a formidable challenge to survival, actually poses little danger for the caribou. The coat that covers their entire body insulates them so well that even in the most extreme temperatures they do not shiver, and require little if any increase in metabolism to maintain their body temperature. Even the muzzle, except for the nostrils, is furred to protect it as the caribou thrusts it into the snow in search of food. The coat consists of long, brittle guard-hairs that taper in both directions from the middle, forming a tight outer layer covering the fine curly wool beneath. The guard-hairs are not truly hollow, as often described, but rather contain large, highly vacuolated cells that serve, along with the wool, to trap warm air next to the body.

The warmth of caribou skins is renowned throughout the North; native peoples have always prized them for clothing and sleeping robes. In many native societies it was even more important to kill caribou for their hides than for meat. Fish or small game might provide alternate food, but in some regions no substitute existed for clothing made of caribou skins, when the icy grip of arctic winter closed.

Caribou possess other physical characteristics that suit them to life in the cold. They have what is called a counter-current circulatory system in their legs. The blood vessels returning from the legs run in close association with arteries carrying warm blood from the body. Thus much of the heat from the warm blood is transferred to the cold blood and returned to the body. This mechanism allows the temperature in the caribou's legs to stay at about 50°F or less, compared with the normal body temperature of almost 105°F. Since the tissues of the legs and hooves are adapted to function at the much lower temperature, the thermal gradient between the legs and the environment is reduced, lessening heat loss through the legs, which are in constant contact with snow for so much of the year. Similar circulatory systems have been discovered in the flippers of sea mammals, the feet of arctic birds, and in other creatures inhabiting cold climates.

Caribou also adapt their activity to the weather. As temperatures fall, they become more active, particularly in feeding. The exertion required to dig for food in the snow helps keep the animals warm, and the added food intake generates heat through fermentation in the rumen. At extremely low temperatures, however, especially in association with windchill, the caribou tend to feed less and spend more time lying curled up to reduce heat loss. They sometimes dig out a bed in the snow, which affords them a measure of protection from the wind, and they may seek sheltered locations. Individuals also bed down closer together during periods of high windchill to use each other's bodies as protection. Nevertheless, even in the most devastating conditions of extreme cold and windchill, caribou may be seen feeding, fuelling their bodies against the great heat-sink of the universe.

If bitter cold hinders the caribou little, snow is a different story. Snow saps their strength as they travel, interferes with feeding, and under certain conditions hinders escape from predators. Indeed, the name caribou comes from the Micmac Indian word *Xalibu,* meaning "the pawer," which describes this animal's habit of digging through the snow to reach buried plants. The name could hardly be more appropriate; caribou spend a greater part of their lives in digging for food beneath the snow than in any other activity.

Deep snow or, worse yet, icy crusts caused by melting and refreezing or freezing rains represent a much greater danger to the caribou than extreme cold. Icy crusts prevent the animals from reaching the low-growing plants that supply their winter food. Studies of caribou from arctic Alaska to Newfoundland provide ample evidence that snow conditions influence the animals' choice of winter range as well as their movements, feeding, and behaviour throughout the winter.

The distribution of major herds varies considerably from winter to winter, depending on both the autumn migration pattern and yearly changes in snow conditions. In choosing a winter range a herd first selects areas that have the shallowest and softest snow. Within this chosen region each group seeks places where food is abundant and the snow particularly easy to dig through. One of the main reasons that most herds of barren-ground caribou leave the tundra to winter is that the soft light snow in the forests is easier to dig through than the wind-packed crusts of the barrens. Yet caribou can winter on the tundra, and in some years large groups of animals that normally go to the forests remain beyond the tree-line. Some populations, such as those on the Arctic Islands and those of the far northern Canadian mainland, never travel to the forests. These tundra-dwellers survive by feeding on ridges blown clear of snow, or in places where they can break the crusts into slabs and paw them aside.

Caribou locate their food by smell. As they walk along, they thrust their noses into the snow searching for favoured plants. These they locate almost unerringly, wasting little energy digging unsuccessful craters. Caribou can easily smell plants through snow less than a foot deep; in deeper snow they usually search near trees, shrubs, or grasses that poke through the surface. The emerging stems provide an air vent that allows the odour from the ground to rise through the otherwise impenetrable blanket. Once food is located, the caribou begin to dig.

The caribou's hoof has evolved as an efficient tool for digging in the snow. A male's front hoof measures five inches in length and is equally broad. The edges are rounded and curve inward at the tip. During winter the hard outer shell of the hoof is no longer being worn away by the rough ground; the hoof therefore becomes concave, with a sharp edge. The caribou use this big specialized hoof both as a pick to break crusts and as a shovel for removing soft or broken snow from their craters. The edges also provide excellent traction on slippery ice. The caribou change their methods of digging to suit the snow conditions. In the soft and shallow snow of early winter they employ a long pawing motion, reaching far forward. Later, crusts form and their digging becomes a faster, downward chopping action, and the broken snow is removed in chunks and pieces.

Feeding craters generally measure a foot and a half or more in diameter at the snow surface, but only a tenth as much is exposed at ground level because fine snow keeps sliding back into the crater, much as sand fills the hole that a child digs at the beach. A caribou eats what it can from one crater and then digs another nearby, usually without overlapping the first. If food plants are distributed abundantly and evenly over the ground, however, instead of in patches, several animals may make a communal crater and feed together. They advance along a front, pawing the snow back behind them into the area where they have already fed.

The feeding animals disturb the snow in a large area around the craters, causing it to harden within a few hours and making subsequent digging there more difficult. After a band uses an area once or twice, it becomes undesirable for further feeding and the animals move on. In this way a herd's own activities protect an area from being over-grazed. The variation in ranges used from winter to winter also distributes grazing pressure and prevents excessive use of one region.

Most caribou bands feed at sunrise and sunset, and rest and ruminate during the middle of the day. In mid-winter they generally forage once during the night as well. On the northernmost ranges beyond the Arctic Circle, there is a period in the winter when the sun never rises at all. Then of course the caribou carry out their activities in darkness, although they still tend to rest during the lightest part of the day when the pale glow of the sun just brightens the southern horizon.

Even though caribou feed among the trees, they move onto frozen lakes, rivers, meadows, or bare ridges to rest and chew their cuds. Moving into the open is a strategy against wolves. Since the caribou's only defence lies in running away, they must see predators approach in time to escape. They lie in compact groups, facing in all directions, alert for any movement against the snow. The wind-packed snow in open areas also offers better footing than the soft powder in the bush, should flight be necessary. If disturbed while feeding in the woods, caribou run into the open. This running away from cover rather than towards it contrasts with the behaviour of other ungulates such as moose and white-tailed deer. Once out of the trees, caribou can see the danger more clearly, bunch up to confuse a pursuing predator, and use their superior speed to best advantage. Thus caribou will not winter in an area unless it offers wide vistas for the detection of predators. They make little use of large unbroken tracts of forest.

In the open, caribou are confident that their fleetness will protect them from their ancestral enemy, the wolf. Resting caribou will usually allow a wolf, human, or vehicle to approach within 200 or 300 yards before they even stand up. They seem to know whether or not a wolf is hunting. Even light aircraft can usually land and taxi close by without alarming them. When they are disturbed, they exhibit great curiosity towards the approaching object, circling downwind with a characteristic trot, tails up, heads held high, testing the wind. Smell is the sense that caribou rely on for definite confirmation of danger. Usually they run off after catching the scent of a predator, rearing on their hind legs just before they flee; but sometimes they behave indecisively, dashing back and forth past the intruder.

The caribou's behaviour towards predators makes them vulnerable to modern hunters with high-powered rifles. They can be approached within easy rifle-shot, and even after a hunter begins shooting, the animals may mill about in confusion and be slow to move off. A hunter can often kill several caribou from a single group. Now that northern hunters travel by snowmobile, the caribou have even less chance of escape. When pursued, they stay in the open; a hunter can keep chasing them as long as he wants. The behaviour that has served the caribou so well for thousands of years in coping with wolves works against them in their confrontations with modern man.

As winter wears on, the caribou move when they need to, seeking the best combination of available food and snow conditions. The shallow snow of early winter impedes the animals little as they travel or feed, so they range widely, foraging wherever food is abundant. Then, as deepening snow restricts their movements, they become relatively sedentary; by mid-winter they may be concentrated in certain regions. The same animals that cover fifteen miles a day at other seasons often take a week to move half that distance during the winter. By February the caribou may be forced to devote twelve hours a day or more to pawing snow aside to feed, each animal digging more than a hundred craters daily to get the ten to fifteen pounds of forage it needs.

If a herd finds particularly abundant or nutritious forage, it will continue to feed in that area even though shallower snow exists elsewhere. For example, the animals of the Central Arctic herd in northern Alaska normally feed for much of the winter in the deep snow of forested river valleys, even though the

windswept ridges nearby are free of snow. Despite the snow, food is relatively more abundant in the forests than on the ridges. Only in late winter, when the snow finally becomes so deep that it requires too much energy to dig in the forests, do the caribou move to the more open but poorer ranges on the slopes.

If the snow becomes strongly crusted, caribou can walk on top to reach lichens growing on the tree branches. The possibility of feeding on tree lichens is probably another reason why barren-ground caribou generally winter in the forests. Such lichens constitute a regular part of the diet of woodland caribou. In the deep snow regions of British Columbia these animals normally make migrations up to the mountains, where deep crusted snow allows them to reach abundant tree lichens.

In winter the caribou's entire metabolism and physiology become geared to poor nutrition. Just as winter is a season of dormancy for the northern landscape, so it brings a kind of dormancy and husbanding of resources among the caribou. Survival becomes a question of conserving energy in every possible way. The caribou's basal metabolic rate drops by twenty-five per cent or more, and all growth ceases from November through to April or May. Despite these adjustments, their condition deteriorates as winter wears on; they cannot obtain as much energy from their food as they expend in all their activities. The animals lose weight as fat deposits on the back, inside the gut cavity, and in the bone marrow are depleted. Adult females and young animals usually decline by about ten per cent by spring, but under extremely difficult conditions the weight loss can exceed twenty per cent. After a winter of deep snow the caribou filing along the spring migration trails look like scarecrows, ribs showing beneath the tattered coats.

Because the caribou are adapted to poor nutrition and the consequent weight loss, they have little difficulty in surviving normal winters. Even during severe winters, mass die-offs are rare. If any members of a herd do starve, they are usually calves or yearlings who have little stored energy and are lowest in the social hierarchy. Exceptions occur in some maritime regions where brief thaws or freezing rains can form icy crusts that seal off the animals' food supply over large areas. Periodic mass starvation attributed to icing conditions has been recorded in the Alaska Peninsula herd, on Coats Island in Hudson Bay, on several of the Canadian Arctic Islands, and in Greenland. The surviving females in these herds may also fail to reproduce for one or more seasons following the winter of starvation. Such catastrophes recur often enough among the populations inhabiting those areas that climate may be considered the factor that controls them.

Perhaps the caribou's most important adaptation to life in the far North is their ability to subsist on lichens, or reindeer moss as it is often erroneously called. These primitive plants grow widely on the poor soils of the boreal forest and tundra, offering a relatively abundant supply of easily digestible energy. The protein content of most lichen species is so low, however, that no other grazing animals can survive on them. Caribou can subsist on lichens because they have developed an efficient mechanism of recycling urea, a waste product in the blood that contains nitrogen. During the winter caribou return sixty per cent or more of their urea to the rumen, where the nitrogen may be used again. Since nitrogen is one of the vital components of protein synthesis, the caribou's ability to recycle waste nitrogen allows them to live on a lower intake of protein than other ungulates.

The caribou's common use of lichens in winter has led to a popular misconception that they depend on these plants. This assumed dependency prompted some biologists in the 1950s and 1960s to argue that forest fires could be causing declines in caribou populations by destroying the lichens on their winter ranges. Lichens grow back slowly following a severe fire and take decades to return to their former abundance. These scientists argued that increased human activity, especially prospecting, resulted in a much higher incidence of fires than under natural conditions. Their arguments convinced government agencies that destruction of winter ranges by fire had resulted in declines in caribou herds and that further reductions were in the offing if forest fires were left uncontrolled. As a result, during the 1960s and most of the 1970s the federal Department of Indian Affairs and Northern Development had a policy of fighting forest fires on wilderness ranges known to be important to caribou. Alaska has also fought fires since the 1940s.

Subsequent studies, however, have revealed several false assumptions in the arguments implicating forest fires in the decline of caribou populations. It is now clear that caribou can thrive on many ranges with few or no lichens at all in their winter food. Caribou on the Alaska Peninsula and the Aleutian Islands, for example, feed almost entirely on sedges. Indeed, rather than depending on lichens, caribou cannot subsist exclusively on them. They need other plants, especially wintergreen varieties such as sedges, horsetails, and low-bush cranberry. Even herds whose normal diet contains a high proportion of lichens eat many other foods. On the ranges of central Canada, where lichens play an important role in sustaining caribou through the winter, it has been shown that lichen stocks far exceed the herds' requirements. Forest fires could become five to ten times more frequent before they would begin to affect the caribou's food supply.

The assumption that increased human populations and activity in the North have accelerated the rate of destruction of caribou range by fire is also erroneous. Naturally caused fires still account for ninety per cent or more of the acreage burned in the boreal forest. Fires started by lightning have raged through northern forests for thousands of years. Fire has now come to be regarded as not only a natural, but a necessary ecological process in the northern forest ecosystem; burning actually helps maintain lichen crops by destroying vascular plants and mosses that would eventually replace lichens in unburned areas. Rather than constituting a threat, fire plays a role in maintaining the diversity of vegetation and habitat so important to the caribou.

During the winter caribou compete with one another for the best feeding spots. The scarcer the food or the more demanding the snow conditions, the greater the competition. As soon as a group fans out to feed, some caribou start to displace others from their craters. Larger, stronger animals usually intimidate smaller rivals by threats or displays of superiority, but sometimes actual fights break out. In late winter a band of feeding caribou presents a scene of continual conflict. The advantages of dominance are clear: a caribou that usurps another's crater gets to feed without having expended the energy to dig away the snow. It gets a free meal. Or the dominant animal may simply be looking for more abundant food or a better place to dig its own crater. Sometimes one caribou will chase another out of its bed, establishing dominance that may be useful in future contests for food.

When a caribou moves to displace a rival, it approaches purposefully, most often from the rear or the side. Usually the aggressor lowers its head and points its antlers at the animal, or it may use a threat similar to that adopted by bulls approaching cows during the rut. The subordinate almost always yields to the aggressor without any contact, and moves off to dig a new crater or to displace another caribou. Sometimes the dominant caribou jabs the retreating animal with its antlers or kicks at it to hurry it on its way. Occasionally, however, the challenger finds an opponent ready to turn and defend its crater. If both caribou still have their antlers, they lock together and fight. The combatants may also rear and kick at each other with their front hooves, especially if they have already shed their antlers.

Who displaces whom depends largely on the relative size of the adversaries and their antlers. In early winter, before the big bulls drop their antlers, they easily dominate cows and younger males. But later on the adult bulls, barren cows, and some younger bulls have shed their antlers; then the pregnant cows, who still retain theirs, become dominant over their antlerless companions. The pregnant females can claim and defend the best feeding areas in late winter, when they especially need high-quality food to nourish their rapidly growing foetuses.

This competition for food during the lean northern winter probably explains why caribou are the only species of deer in which females possess antlers, and why pregnant cows retain them after bulls and barren cows have shed theirs. The dominance achieved by the antlered pregnant females gives the greatest chance of survival to the productive members of the herd, and may also account for the usual separation of males and females during the winter. The observation that bulls occupy different ranges from the cow-juvenile groups in winter has led to the hypothesis that they can tolerate deeper snow than the smaller animals, and therefore exploit ranges avoided by the others. Such behaviour seems too altruistic, however, for voluntary withdrawal to marginal areas would be disadvantageous to the bulls. More likely, the antlered cows defend the best ranges and force the males into more difficult snow conditions. There is another possible explanation. Since wolves prey primarily on young animals, the packs concentrate on the ranges used by the cows and their accompanying calves and yearlings. By withdrawing from the areas occupied by the young, the big bulls enjoy a somewhat reduced danger from predation.

The social dominance of antlered females in late winter also protects their calves. Calves assume the social status of their mothers. Cows drive off any caribou that behave aggressively towards their calves, so the young ones get to feed in the best places with their mothers. If left alone, the calves would find themselves at the bottom of the social hierarchy, since they are the smallest and weakest members of the herd. An antlered cow thus increases the chances of survival for both the calf she already has and the one growing inside her.

Protection from other caribou is just one of several advantages that a calf gains by staying with its mother through the first winter. It also benefits by feeding in the craters she digs. This spares the small animal the energy required to dig for itself. Sometimes mother and young feed side by side in the same crater, but often the calf actually displaces the cow by bunting her in the side or searching for her udder. Since the cow no longer wants to allow the calf to nurse, she steps aside and the calf claims the crater. The incidence of calves displacing cows seems to increase in late winter, when the snow is deep and the energy-saving of greatest value.

By following its mother, the calf learns the local movements of the herd, which lead it to the best snow conditions and most abundant food. The calf benefits from its mother's alertness and experience in avoiding predators and also ensures that its activities will be synchronized with the group, especially during pursuit by wolves. Synchrony within a band has been clearly shown to constitute a defence against predation, and animals that behave differently or stand out in the herd are vulnerable.

Then at winter's end, the bond of the calves to their mothers plays one last vital role. When the cows heed the urge of spring and set out for their distant calving grounds, their young follow. And as the calves trail along, the migratory tradition — the age-old routes and rhythm of travel, so fundamental to the life of barren-ground caribou — is passed on from one generation to the next.

WINTER PHOTOGRAPHS

Pages 132-133: Bull caribou crossing the Blackstone River, Yukon. Soon after the rut, the big bulls withdraw once again from the cows and young animals.

Page 136: Antlers of a big bull killed near Courageous Lake, Northwest Territories.

Page 137: Antlerless bull in black spruce forest, East Fork, Chandalar River, Alaska. The big bulls shed their antlers soon after the rut.

Pages 138-139: The cows withdraw to their winter ranges, Ogilvie Mountains, Yukon.

Page 140: A caribou feeds in the bottom of a crater that it has just dug, Old Crow, Yukon.

Page 141: Two antlerless animals lay back their ears as they prepare to rear and kick at each other in competition for a feeding place. Old Crow, Yukon.

Pages 142-143: Willow ptarmigan foraging for buds, Yellowknife, Northwest Territories.

Page 145: Caribou in typical winter habitat, Arseno Lake, Northwest Territories.

Pages 146-147: Flight is the caribou's method of escape from predators. Mattberry Lake, Northwest Territories.

Page 148: A cow chases another caribou from its feeding crater, near Old Crow, Yukon.

Pages 150-151: At the end of winter a caribou grazes on newly exposed vegetation, Bathurst Inlet, Northwest Territories.

Page 152 (upper): On open ridges caribou feed and rest in the same areas. Schaeffer Mountain, Yukon.

Page 152 (lower): Winter range of the Bathurst herd, near Great Slave Lake, Northwest Territories.

Page 153 (upper): Caribou digging for food, Old Crow, Yukon.

Page 153 (lower): Feeding craters, Mattberry Lake, Northwest Territories. Caribou rely on their sense of smell to locate food beneath the snow; then they dig craters to reach it.

Page 154: Caribou trails and beds on a lake in the winter range of the Bathurst herd, Northwest Territories.

Page 155 (upper left): These caribou exhibit typical curiosity towards a possible predator, near Coppermine River, Northwest Territories.

Page 155 (upper right): Caribou running on Mattberry Lake, Northwest Territories.

Page 155 (lower left): A wolf carries the hind leg of a caribou away from a kill site, Arseno Lake, Northwest Territories.

Page 155 (lower right): A hunter unloads caribou from his sled after a hunting trip by snowmobile, Coppermine, Northwest Territories.

Page 156: Two young bulls spar playfully in late winter, Mattberry Lake, Northwest Territories.

Part II

Men and herds on the barren-lands

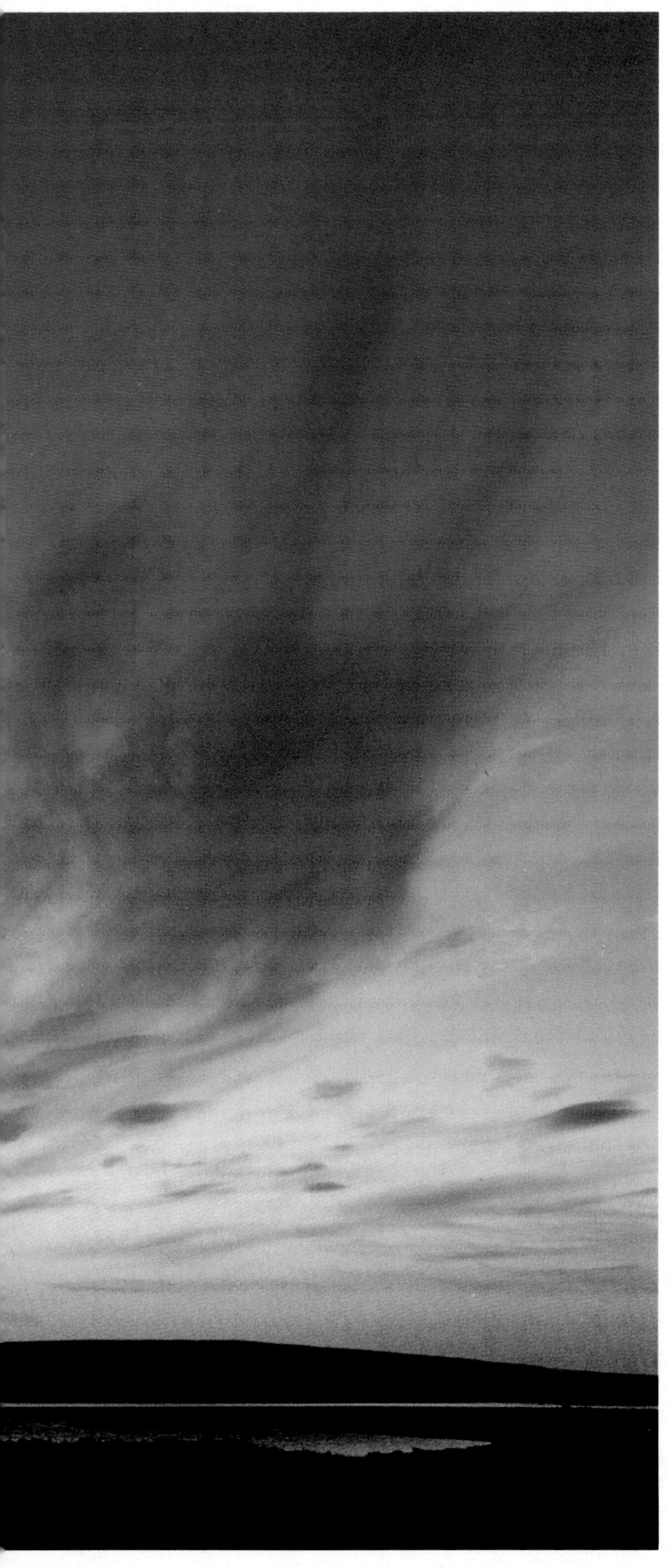

The bones of the men who painted them have long since turned to dust. But the vivid depictions of wild reindeer, hidden in darkness for 15,000 years on the walls of the caverns of Europe, have come down to us, a beautiful expression of the reverence felt by the Cro-Magnon hunters for the animals that gave them life.

These earliest human artists were by no means the first people to depend on the herds of the tundra. Fossil remains of caribou occur prominently with all paleolithic cultures of Europe, beginning with the Neanderthals over 40,000 years ago. Thus men have fed and clothed themselves by hunting caribou since the middle of the ice age, even before we became *Homo sapiens.*

Throughout the northern circumpolar lands the story is the same: caribou have formed the basis of most arctic and sub-arctic cultures. Indeed, in many areas of the North human life would have been impossible without the caribou. Some peoples such as the Chipewyan Indians and the Caribou Eskimos depended on these animals for virtually all necessities of life. Caribou supplied not only meat for humans and dogs, but also fat for light and cooking, hides for tents, boat covers, sleeping robes, and footwear, and bone for needles, scrapers, fish hooks, and a variety of weapons.

The hunting peoples who lived almost completely on caribou needed to kill many animals to fill all their needs: fifty or more per person each year. Of course, each individual did not require the meat from fifty caribou, but many animals were killed in late summer to obtain short-haired skins for clothing, before the weather was cold enough to preserve the meat. Much meat spoiled, and more animals had to be killed later for food. Where marine mammals, fish, or other game such as moose, mountain sheep, or musk-oxen could provide alternate food, fewer caribou were required.

The recent European explorers of northern Canada and Alaska were also forced to rely upon caribou during their travels. The vastness of the arctic and sub-arctic wilderness made it impossible to carry all supplies required on extended trips. Northern travellers counted on living off the land; that meant hunting caribou. When the animals failed to appear as expected, the expeditions ended tragically. Sir John Franklin lost half his men in 1821, while returning from Bathurst Inlet to Winter Lake through a tundra region that should have yielded many caribou. Just over a century later John Hornby and his two companions set out to winter on the Thelon River. They planned to meet the autumn migration of the Beverly herd to secure their winter meat. When delays caused them to miss the southward passage of the caribou, their fates were sealed. They had no dogs to cover wide areas in search of game. Their lingering deaths by starvation provided a grim reminder of the price paid for miscalculating the ways of the caribou.

Even such an enduring enterprise as the northern fur trade owed its existence to the caribou. Individual trappers on the land relied upon the herds, and the traders at isolated posts obtained much of their food through hunting and fishing. Many fur trade settlements, from York Factory on Hudson Bay to St. Michael on the Bering Sea, were established along migration paths of the caribou.

Before the coming of Europeans, who distributed firearms, native hunters employed two major methods of killing the large numbers of caribou they required: either they speared them as the animals swam rivers or lakes at traditional water crossings, or they built corrals to entrap migrating caribou, which they then killed with snares, spears, or bows and arrows.

Spearing at water crossings was a simple and efficient hunting method practised by Indians and Eskimos alike, both on the tundra and within the boreal forest. Hunters in a kayak or canoe intercepted caribou swimming a river or a narrows in a lake, and speared them through the exposed back with short sharp lances so as to injure the spinal cord or dorsal aorta or puncture the chest cavity. Since caribou float for a long time after being killed, the hunters could pursue and attack the band as long as it remained in the water, without having to stop to retrieve dead animals.

Often long rows of stone cairns that the Eskimos called *inuksuit* (meaning "resembling a person") were used to lead migrating caribou to crossings suitable for ambush. The animals apparently perceived these stone men as lines of hunters and would not pass through. Often hunters stationed themselves between the *inuksuit* to heighten the illusion. Where suitable water crossings were not available, the hunters used *inuksuit* to direct migrating caribou into ambushes where the hunters shot them with bows and arrows. Mute lines of stone men, the abandoned shooting pits where the hunters once hid, and perhaps an arrowhead here and there may still be seen on the barrens today, silent testimony to a vanished way of life.

Indian hunters in the northern forest constructed fences of trees and brush held together by spruce or willow roots, to direct caribou into an oblong corral. These drift fences, up to several miles in length, gradually converged into the narrow opening of the corral. When a band of caribou entered the wings of the drift fences, the hidden hunters moved in behind, drove them into the corral, and blocked the entrance with cut trees. Inside the corral a maze of hedges was set, with snares in the openings. Any animals that escaped the snares were killed by hunters with bows and arrows or spears. Variations on such fences and corrals were used in many areas of Alaska, the Yukon, and in the forested areas of the Northwest Territories.

Hunting at water crossings or with fences and corrals was a communal affair. Hunters and their families, as many as several hundred people, assembled at the most productive places. Late summer and early autumn were the favoured times of the hunt.

When a major migration passed, hundreds, even thousands, of caribou were slaughtered in a few days. Then the work began. Precious hides had to be staked out to dry, skin side up, and scraped of all flesh and tissue: the soft-furred skins of calves for underclothing and boot liners, the bull hides for sleeping skins and tents, and the tough-haired skins of the lower legs for footwear. Meat was cut into strips to dry in the sun or over smoky fires; if the weather was cold enough, fresh meat was cached. The long sheaths of shiny sinew stripped off the back muscles were split and twisted into strong sewing thread. Blocks of white tallow, cut from the rumps of the bulls, served as fuel for stone lamps. Fat was also mixed with dried meat to make pemmican. And all the while everyone feasted on the choicest and richest parts: fresh livers, hearts, kidneys, and tongues, soup made from heads, and roasted ribs and marrow bones.

The hunters employed similar methods to make kills during the spring migration. The spring hunt was of less significance than the one in autumn, however, for the caribou would arrive in poor condition after the winter. They carried little fat, and their hides were riddled with breathing holes of warble fly larvae, making them worthless for clothing. Warm weather followed soon after the migration, so all meat had to be dried or it would spoil. Moreover, water crossings usually remained frozen at the time of spring migration and thus hunters could not spear swimming animals. If the spring hunt failed, it often mattered little; soon fish and migrating birds became available as alternate food. If the hunters killed caribou in the spring, they often took only the few parts still containing fat, such as the heads and tongues or the unborn foetuses, which were considered a special delicacy.

Hunting peoples who depended on caribou had to predict accurately where the migrations would pass, and arrive there at the right time. Such anticipation demanded an intimate knowledge of the country and the behaviour of the animals. When caribou were numerous, the hunting peoples could be confident that the animals would arrive at traditional places. Bellies were full and life was good. Even if the main herd failed to appear as anticipated, sizeable bands of stragglers passed through in sufficient numbers for the hunters to get by. But when caribou grew scarce, the routes of the migrations became much less predictable. Life became haunted with doubt; the spectre of starvation stalked the land. Then the decision of where to hunt became a matter of life and death. To wait at a crossing to which caribou never came meant hardship or death.

Periodic starvation or emigration were part of the way of life of northern hunting peoples. They probably faced a major crisis every two or three generations because of recurring fluctuations in caribou populations. A tribe confronted with declining numbers of caribou and the resulting irregular migration patterns had but two choices: either they moved out, searching for alternate game, or they starved. In this way human hunters were no different from other predators whose distribution and abundance depend on their prey. If they over-exploited the caribou in their region, they in turn declined, allowing the herd time to recover.

To help overcome the uncertainty of intercepting migrating caribou, some hunting peoples established elaborate social-territorial organizations and kinship relationships, which distributed the population of hunters across a wide front. This strategy maximized the chances of at least one group intercepting a major migration, and ensured the sharing of provender when a kill was made. The "caribou-eater" Chipewyans, who inhabited the northern forests and the edge of the barren-lands from Hudson Bay to Great Slave Lake, exemplified such a society.

Chipewyan hunting groups, consisting of two or more closely related families, spaced themselves along the tree-line, which runs roughly perpendicular to the routes of the migrating caribou. Although the hunters tended to concentrate in areas where they expected caribou on the basis of recent experience, they always dispersed widely enough that one or more hunting groups was likely to encounter the migration. The successful hunters killed as many caribou as they could, usually far more than they themselves needed, so that a surplus was available to share with those who had failed to secure any. This sharing of the necessities of life was promoted by the Chipewyan kinship system and marriage custom. Marriages were always arranged between members of different hunting groups, and all kin of the spouses then became kin. Marriage custom also required a hunter to perform bride service in the hunting area of his wife's parents; thus men grew familiar with other hunting ranges. Members of nearby groups visited regularly, maintaining a network of relationships that ensured the free and continual exchange of information concerning the movements of the caribou. When kills were made, the take had to be shared with any less fortunate hunters.

It is interesting to compare the strategies developed by human hunters with the methods used by the wolf, the other great predator of the caribou. Northern peoples did not attempt to and could not follow the caribou: the herds moved too quickly and too far. Instead they depended upon killing hundreds of animals when large herds arrived each spring and fall. Such surplus killing was a necessity for any group dependent on migratory caribou. When the caribou appeared, the hunters had to take all they could get against the times when the herds were gone. When kills were made for hides in late summer, before the weather was cold enough to freeze the meat, it spoiled. Such waste could not be helped. It was an unquestioned part of life.

Wolves, on the other hand, have always hunted by remaining in contact with the herds. They follow the migrating caribou, losing contact only when they den to have their pups. Wolves hunt caribou throughout the year, and rarely kill more than a few animals at any one time.

For thousands of years men and wolves co-existed on the barren-lands, each pursuing the caribou in its own way. Although both hunted caribou, and in many areas depended almost exclusively on them, neither displaced the other. Then in less than a generation, mechanized transportation and the high-powered rifle revolutionized human hunting. Northern hunters now pursue the herds year-round as the wolf has always done. The ancient relationship between men and herds on the barren-lands has been altered forever. In the past the comings and goings of the caribou determined the survival of human hunters in the North. Today it is human hunters who control the destiny of the caribou.

Hunters can now locate the herds anywhere, even in the vastness of the barren-lands. The use of aircraft to spot the caribou has removed the uncertainty about where the migrations will pass. Radios relay the information from camp to camp. Hunting parties cover hundreds of miles by aircraft, snowmobile, or outboard motorboat. The caribou cannot escape such hunters.

Northern peoples are no longer subject to the same ecological laws that affect populations of other predators. They no longer rely exclusively on the resources of the land. They no longer starve or emigrate when caribou become scarce, allowing the depleted herds time to recover. The balance between predator and prey has tipped entirely in favour of the modern, technologically-equipped hunter. Unless hunting is controlled, the great herds of barren-ground caribou will be destroyed.

The crash of the Western Arctic herd provides the best example of how quickly excessive hunting can bring down a large and healthy caribou population. This herd was once the largest in North America, ranging over 175,000 miles of tundra and mountains in northwestern Alaska. In 1970 it numbered about a quarter of a million animals. No one believed that the hunters from the native villages that lay scattered over this huge wilderness could possibly endanger such a throng. No restrictions were placed on hunting: caribou could be killed anywhere, anytime, in any numbers, by anyone. Indeed, some biologists felt that a herd so large must be in danger of over-grazing its range, and they encouraged local hunters to take as many caribou as possible.

Each autumn the Western Arctic herd ran the gauntlet of communities along the Bering Sea coast and in the western Brooks Range, and then wintered within snowmobile distance of several villages. The number of caribou killed mounted each year: twenty thousand, twenty-five thousand, thirty thousand, possibly more. These statistics included only those animals brought to the villages. There were many reports of caribou killed and abandoned, of groups slaughtered for only the choicest parts, of uncounted animals carelessly wounded and left to wander and die a lingering death. Still no one worried. The Alaska Department of Fish and Game did not even consider it worthwhile to conduct another census of the herd until 1975.

The results of that survey shocked everyone interested in Alaska's wildlife. Only about 100,000 animals remained. The general reaction was to disbelieve the count; surely there must have been an error. Nothing was done to reduce the killing. Another 25,000 animals were slaughtered the following winter. The next summer the census estimated only 65,000 caribou. Now there could be no doubt: the supposedly invincible herd was in rapid decline.

The crash of the Western Arctic herd dramatized the plight of Alaska's caribou because it was the largest herd in the state; but other major Alaskan herds had already suffered serious declines. In the mid-1960s the Fortymile herd numbered 50,000 animals, and the Nelchina herd was over 60,000 strong. Both these herds crossed roads during their annual migrations. Each autumn when word passed along that caribou were nearing the highways, hunters from Fairbanks, Anchorage, and other towns drove out to "get their caribou." Firing lines formed along the roads. The hills echoed with the scream of two-cycle engines as snowmobiles and all-terrain vehicles carried hunters to the animals. By 1973 all that remained of the Fortymile herd was a remnant of about 5000 animals; the Nelchina could boast no more than twice that number. In just ten years, between 1965 and 1975, Alaska lost over half its caribou.

The Alaska Department of Fish and Game belatedly realized that the state's caribou populations could not survive the combined onslaught of mechanized hunting and uncontrolled predators. With their low reproductive rates, caribou are ill-equipped to replace heavy losses to their populations. In an attempt to halt the decline and allow the herds to recover, the department severely restricted or completely banned hunting on several herds, and moved to reduce wolf populations.

These measures produced a remarkable recovery among the caribou, typified by the resurgence of the Western Arctic herd. Beginning in 1977 the department issued a total of 3000 permits, for bull caribou only, for the entire range of the herd. The permits were apportioned among the communities according to need. The department also opened aerial hunting of wolves on parts of the herd's range, a practice that had been widespread in Alaska during the 1960s but outlawed in the 1970s. Two fortuitous events also helped: the caribou began wintering in areas remote from the largest villages, and diseases further reduced the wolf population.

Given this respite from predation by both humans and wolves, the herd began to increase at a rate of twenty per cent a year. Survival of calves improved dramatically. By the summer of 1980 the herd numbered 140,000 or more. At this rate of increase the herd's doubling time is less than five years, and the herd should again number a quarter of a million animals by 1985.

With the upturn of the fortunes of the Western Arctic herd, the hunting quotas are being increased, and there is every prospect of even greater allowable yields as the herd continues to grow. The people of the region are already benefiting from the short period of restricted hunting. Other Alaskan herds are also on the road to recovery.

Unfortunately, the barren-ground caribou of the Northwest Territories are still suffering the same sort of slaughters that ravaged the Alaskan herds. The figures speak for themselves. The Bathurst herd, which numbered 200,000 or more in 1971, has dropped to half that total. The Beverly herd has been reduced by 65,000 animals in the same period; during the winter of 1979-1980 alone over 15,000 animals were killed from this herd. The Kaminuriak herd has dropped from 63,000 in 1968 to fewer than 40,000 in 1980. Two decades earlier the herd numbered at least 150,000 and probably much higher. From the ranges of all these herds come annual stories of the same damaging and wasteful hunting practices that occurred in Alaska.

It may be asked, "If caribou co-existed for tens of thousands of years with wolves and native hunters, why are they suddenly endangered?" The answer is that the natural cycles that reduced hunting of the herds when they fell to low levels no longer occur. The human populations with their newly acquired capabilities of locating and killing caribou no longer starve or emigrate if the herds in their regions begin to decline. Although the survival of the northern native peoples no longer depends on the comings and goings of the herds, caribou meat still provides a valuable source of food for many northern communities, the food preferred above all others. The descendants of men who once drew life from the herds still think of themselves as caribou hunters. They know that hunting is the proper pursuit of man. So they keep on hunting, driving the herds to lower and lower levels.

Among the native peoples the age-old hunting instincts have not died. It is almost impossible for outsiders to grasp the fundamental importance of the hunt in native societies, almost impossible to understand how much they equate the abundant killing of caribou with survival and happiness. Because the modern technological society has come to the North so suddenly, the instincts evolved over thousands of years have not had time to adjust. The people of Baker Lake and Eskimo Point, who now go out by snowmobile with high-powered rifles to get their caribou, were starving twenty years ago because they could not kill enough. To now be told that taking this abundance will destroy the animals they cherish, the animals that have always sustained them, is more than they can bear.

Therefore it is not surprising that native peoples oppose restrictions on hunting with all their political resources. Caribou hunting lies at the very well-springs of their identity. Native peoples see restrictions on the ancient hunting traditions as yet another, and particularly deadly, example of the destruction of their culture by an alien society. To give up their right to hunt freely is to give up one of the bases of their way of life; yet if they do not, they are told they will destroy the caribou.

Native peoples face a tragic dilemma. It would be desirable for any measures for the management of caribou to be implemented slowly, allowing time for education and discussion, and for a trust to develop between the native hunters and the wildlife biologists that both have the best interests of the caribou at heart. But there is no time to wait. If present trends continue, the Bathurst, Beverly, and Kaminuriak herds will be wiped out in five to ten years — probably not extinct, but pitiful remnants of the great herds that today roam the barren-lands, and incapable of supporting any subsistence hunting. The caribou of Southampton Island were exterminated by hunters in the 1920s, and it was only a complete ban of hunting that saved the musk-oxen of Canada from extinction sixty years ago. It would be short-sighted and misguided beneficence to allow uncontrolled hunting to continue for a few more years and then have to close all hunting completely for decades in the hope that the depleted herds could rebuild their numbers.

Although native peoples confront a difficult choice, the situation is far from hopeless. If they considerably curtailed their hunting now, and if wolves were reduced in numbers, the caribou herds would increase quickly. It could be expected that most herds of the Northwest Territories would double within five to six years if hunting were limited to one or two per cent of the herd, mostly bulls. At this rate of increase the Bathurst herd could number half a million animals within ten years, the Beverly 300,000 to 400,000, and the Kaminuriak 150,000. Then such large populations could yield tens of thousands of animals each year on a sustained basis, if wolves were kept in check. Nor do these figures represent the upper limits for the herds. The Bathurst and Beverly herds could possibly support a million caribou each, with half that many in the Kaminuriak herd. Action delayed by just a few years, however, would make the recovery time to reach such numbers much longer.

Admittedly, a great reduction in hunting caribou for several years would cause hardship in many native communities; but the long-range benefits far outweigh these difficulties. A few years of curtailed hunting are certainly preferable to destroying the herds and, as the history of the Western Arctic herd shows, if hunting is strictly controlled the results come quickly. By imposing the necessary restrictions on their own hunting, the native peoples could benefit both themselves and the caribou without any aid or permission from the government. But if they keep on hunting at current levels, they will only ensure the demise of the herds. Then it will be the caribou-hunting peoples who suffer most.

There will also be opposition to the killing of wolves as a method of promoting recovery in the caribou herds. But those against wolf control must accept the sobering thought that the only way to extirpate the wolf from the barren-lands would be to eliminate the caribou. The wolves of the Canadian tundra depend exclusively on caribou: the lower their numbers, the fewer wolves. Only large herds can support substantial populations of wolves. If human hunting and wolf predation together wipe out the caribou, then the wolves will follow them into oblivion. Even before the last caribou was shot on Southampton Island, the wolves had vanished. On Alaska's Kenai Peninsula the story was the same. The wolf populations must be lowered to allow the herds to build up to larger numbers that once again can sustain many wolves as well as the required human hunting.

We cannot have natural wolf populations as well as uncontrolled caribou hunting without accepting population cycles among the caribou. The history of barren-ground caribou herds is one of increases and decreases. There is little doubt that wolves control the numbers of caribou. Wolves usually maintain themselves at a level at which they take the sustainable yield of the herds; the normal ratio is approximately one wolf for every hundred caribou. If humans take many additional animals, the herds decline. Perhaps the early hunting peoples prospered only when the herds were large as a result of periods of low wolf populations. For example, epidemics of rabies and distemper periodically ravage wolf populations; when these occurred in the past, the caribou were granted a respite from predation and their numbers increased. During such times human hunters enjoyed abundance. As the wolves recovered, and if human hunting remained high, the caribou began to decline again, thus initiating another cycle. If we want to start the caribou herds of the Northwest Territories on the road to recovery now, wolves must be controlled. Even when the caribou herds build up to large populations, wolves will have to be controlled continually to hold their numbers below the ratio of one wolf for a hundred caribou. Otherwise, human hunting will start another decline.

Control of wolves does not mean exterminating them; nor does it mean massive poisoning programmes that indiscriminately kill hundreds of wolverines, foxes, weasels, ravens, and jays. Selective shooting from the air can achieve whatever degree of control is necessary, without causing suffering among other wildlife. Hunting of wolves by native peoples would be even better than government control programmes, because sale of the pelts would provide a valuable source of income during the period of restrictions on caribou hunting.

As long as caribou are plentiful, there is little danger of exterminating the wolf. At ratios of one wolf for every 200 or 300 caribou, there would still be many wolves associated with large caribou herds. If it were thought desirable at any time to allow the wolf populations to increase, they could do so very rapidly. Wolves have a much higher potential rate of increase than do caribou. Wolves mature at one year of age and may give birth at two; litters are large, averaging four to six pups. In contrast, female caribou rarely mature before three years of age and give birth to only one calf each year. While wolves can rebuild their populations quickly from very low numbers, caribou cannot.

The story of the Nelchina caribou herd provides an example of how rapidly wolves can increase relative to their prey. In 1953 the Nelchina basin supported 40,000 caribou but only about a dozen wolves: seven years of government predator control and bounty hunting had all but wiped out the packs. Then the area was closed to wolf hunting. By 1965 the Nelchina range supported 425 wolves, but the peak in the caribou population was only 71,000. In other words, the wolf population had increased – whether by reproduction or by immigration – thirty-five times in a period during which the caribou had not even doubled. When the wolves reached peak numbers, only about ten per cent of the caribou calves survived each year; before that, seventy per cent had survived. Soon after 1965 the Nelchina herd crashed.

Wolf control is often criticized on the grounds that the quality of caribou herds would suffer without predators to cull the sick, injured, and old. This concept of the wolf as "shepherd of the flock," killing only the weak and doomed to die, has captured the popular imagination over the past two decades. Unfortunately, it is largely false. There are simply not enough injured and sick animals in a caribou herd to feed the wolves. Wolves' prey consists above all of healthy young animals, those that would become productive members of the herd if they survived. Moreover, the northern environment is harsh enough, with its blizzards, treacherous river crossings, and other hazards, to weed out the weaklings. Wolves were eliminated seventy-five years ago in Newfoundland; yet the caribou herds there are healthy and productive today.

The best possible use of the vast reaches of tundra and northern forests is to support large herds of barren-ground caribou that can yield abundance for the hunter. Wolves also have a right to survive as part of the wholeness of life; the howl of a pack beneath the glittering stars in the arctic night embodies the mystery and wild beauty of the northern lands. And wolves will survive, as long as there are caribou for them to hunt. But neither wolves nor caribou hunters can thrive without the great herds that sustain them. Unless we control both wolves and human hunting, the caribou will vanish and with them the hunters — human and wolf.

The fact that human hunting and wolf predation together pose a serious and immediate threat to the caribou may come as a surprise to those who have been led to believe that pipelines, roads, mining exploration, and other recent industrial developments in the North constituted the major threats to the herds. But it is a fact that northern industrial activities have so far had a minor effect on the caribou, and relatively few restrictions would go far towards protecting caribou from such harmful effects in the near future.

The calving grounds must be protected above all. The launching of the new generation takes place every year on these traditional areas encompassing only a small fraction of each herd's range. Here the environmental conditions are most favourable for the survival of the young. At the time of birth cows are more wary than at any other season; they will flee if disturbed and try to lead their calves away, even before the young ones are dry and steady on their feet. Any concentrated human activity on the calving grounds would interfere with the cow's all-important early maternal behaviour: cleaning the calf, nursing, and forming the vital cow-calf bond. If cows abandoned the traditional calving grounds for less favourable areas, fewer calves would survive. Therefore the calving grounds of all the herds should be made inviolable wildlife sanctuaries, off-limits to all industrial activity and transportation corridors.

Northern roads, railroads, and other transportation routes should be planned to avoid caribou migrations. Where the migrations do cross roads, traffic may have to be convoyed or restricted to certain periods of the day; caribou will travel across roads providing traffic is not too frequent. It has been noted that caribou herds have always declined after roads bisected their ranges, but it was not the roads that caused these losses: it was the hunting. Therefore it is imperative to ban hunting within several miles of all highways and winter roads. Caribou are too vulnerable for hunters to be allowed easy access to them.

Nor can the harassment of caribou with vehicles of any sort — including aircraft — be permitted. It will do little good, however, to restrict the normal use of aircraft and vehicles while allowing hunters to use them to chase caribou. Pursuing caribou with snowmobiles is undoubtedly the most destructive of all forms of human harassment; yet hunting from snowmobiles is still legal in most areas of the North. Hunters often run the animals for long distances in cold weather, causing respiratory disorders as well as the loss of precious energy, and calves may become separated from their mothers. The caribou perceive the snowmobile as a predator pursuing them — which it is — and wolves have conditioned them over thousands of years to flee from pursuit. The caribou cannot adapt to snowmobiles, as they may to other disturbances such as aircraft overflight.

Caribou are not sensitive and delicate creatures that will vanish at the first stress imposed by northern development. They have proved themselves remarkably resilient and adaptable animals. They have endured and prospered during the climatic and geological turmoil of the ice age, evolving to live in environments too severe for all other deer. Caribou still migrate past human settlements despite heavy hunting and harassment. Sometimes they have to be chased off village airstrips so that planes can land. They cross roads and railways and even travel along them. The great herds will continue to flow like a river of life across the barren-lands. . .if we give them a chance.

But if men continue to hunt without regard for the productive capacity of the herds; if at last the North becomes criss-crossed by highways, railroads, pipelines, and high-tension lines; if petro-chemical plants spew out sulphur dioxide that kills the lichens; if the boreal forest is cut for pulpwood and fence posts; if the last wild rivers are dammed and diverted, then the caribou will disappear. There is a limit to the adaptability of even the most resourceful species.

I am haunted by the words of Nuligak, an Eskimo hunter

at last grown too old for the hunt:

When one is no longer able to go hunting
How beautiful the mountains seem to be.
Brooks with their crystal clear water!
A roast on a fire of moss!
It is summer. . . the mosquitoes are gone!
One is happy to live!

Out in the open
The open fire grills the meat.
Its fat sizzles and sings
As it flows upon the stone. . .
How I yearn to be there again!
As these, my own words, so lure me.

They always seem to me the thoughts not just of one man, but of all men as we grow more and more estranged from the natural world.

Barren-ground caribou are creatures of the wilderness and of the ice-age winter. They have survived the vicissitudes of half a million years. The forces of ice and snow that changed the face of the land shaped and strengthened the caribou. So is man a wilderness creature; we too strove and survived against the ice and the weather, and the change. The wilderness formed our most valued and uniquely human characteristics. One does not destroy the place from which he has sprung except at great peril. Unless we understand these things, we will not do what is right for the caribou, or for ourselves.

Selected bibliography

In telling the story of the caribou of Canada and Alaska, I have drawn heavily on the writings of many others. The publications listed here represent only a small fraction of the large and ever-growing body of literature on caribou and their habitat, but they are among those that I have found most useful. Many represent major works that include reviews and summaries of previous studies. The reader who consults these references and their bibliographies will be well on his way to familiarity with what has been discovered about the ecology of caribou.

The vivid paintings left behind in the caves of Europe by the Cro-Magnon hunters more than 15,000 years ago provide the earliest record of man's interest in the caribou. The fascinating story of the rediscovery of these prehistoric masterpieces is recounted by Brown (1928), and several books are available that reproduce the cave art (Moulin, 1965; Lommel, 1966; Powell, 1966; and Sieveking, 1979).

The written history of caribou in North America begins with the narratives of the arctic explorers, who often had to rely on these animals for food and clothing during their overland travels. Martin Frobisher was probably the first European to see and describe caribou in the New World (Best, 1938), and thereafter virtually every major northern expedition produced some accounts of these arctic deer and their use by native peoples. Much information may be gained from the writings of Hearne (1795), Franklin (1823), Richardson (1829), Pike (1892), and Stefansson (1913). Since caribou played a role in the northern fur trade, the journals of the Hudson's Bay Company also contain valuable records of the distribution and abundance of the herds over wide areas.

Formal studies of the biology of barren-ground caribou did not begin until well into the twentieth century, when Murie (1935) studied the herds of Alaska and the Yukon Territory, and Clarke (1940) collected information on the caribou of central Canada. Restricted as they were to the ancient modes of travel – canoe, dog team, snowshoes, and their own two feet – these first caribou biologists were hampered by their inability to follow for very long the ever-moving herds. The difficulty of accurately estimating the number of caribou in vast tracts of wilderness also frustrated them. As Clarke commented with delightful irony, "It is to be hoped that there will never be so few caribou that it will be possible to count them." But with the advent of the bush plane, which allowed large regions to be covered quickly, the caribou began to yield up their secrets; at last the uncountable could be counted. Banfield (1954) published his pioneering studies of the ecology of barren-ground caribou in Canada, which included the first aerial census of the major herds. Similar surveys were undertaken in Alaska by Scott, Chatelain, and Elkins (1950). Banfield (1961) also analyzed the taxonomy of caribou and reindeer, establishing the currently accepted sub-species.

Once aerial surveys had revealed the migration patterns and the calving grounds of the herds, more detailed studies of caribou biology became possible. Skoog (1968) produced a monumental thesis on the ecology of caribou in Alaska, drawing upon twelve years of research that took him to virtually every area of the state. His bibliography, listing over 450 titles, provides the key to a wealth of interesting information. At the same time Kelsall (1968) reported on the decade-long studies of barren-ground caribou by the Canadian Wildlife Service. These two works give comprehensive information on every aspect of caribou ecology and behaviour.

Detailed studies of caribou behaviour during all seasons have now been carried out. Lent (1966) and Pruitt (1960) have described the caribou's calving behaviour and the early maternal care of the calf. Lent also discusses the social behaviour of the caribou, particularly during the post-calving aggregation. His description of a completely open and structureless herd contrasts with the suggestions made by Miller (1974) and Miller et al. (1975) that smaller social groups exist within the great herds.

Roby (1978) and Curatolo (1975) have quantitatively recorded the activities of caribou during the summer, and provide especially good descriptions of how mosquitoes, warble flies, and nose bots affect the herds. Roby's thesis continues the account of the activity budget of the Central Arctic herd throughout the yearly cycle, and contains many valuable hypotheses about how caribou behaviour at all seasons is adaptive to the northern environment. Bergerud (1974a) also describes the role played by various environmental factors in moulding the caribou's behaviour.

Bergerud (1974b) has made the most detailed record of the caribou rut. Although he observed woodland caribou, all the major behaviour patterns of the barren-ground caribou are similar. Lent's paper (1965) on the rut of caribou in the Western Arctic herd may be consulted for differences between the two sub-species.

The terrible cold and long dark periods that characterize the caribou ranges in winter have long hampered studies at that season. Pruitt's pioneering study (1959) revealed the major role that snow plays in the life of the caribou. Henshaw (1968) and

LaPerriere and Lent (1977) have conducted similar studies. The work of Stardom (1975) and Edwards and Ritcey (1959) may be used to compare the wintering behaviour of woodland caribou with that of barren-ground caribou. Miller (1976) elaborated on Pruitt's work and has studied the changes in the caribou's diet throughout the winter, as well as the effect of forest fires on the plant communities on the winter range. Thing (1977) has analyzed the mechanics of the caribou's digging for food in the snow, including calculations of the energy expended in obtaining food through snow of varying depth and hardness. The social behaviour of wintering caribou has been studied by Shea (1978), who provides a good discussion of the value of the bond between cow and calf during the first year of life.

Dauphiné's paper (1976) on the Kaminuriak herd gives a quantitative picture of the growth, reproduction, and the annual energy cycle of the animals of a typical herd. Those seeking information on caribou parasites and diseases may consult the extensive bibliography on this subject compiled by Neiland and Dukeminier (1972).

Wolves have preyed on caribou for tens of thousands of years, and are without doubt the most important selective factor in the caribou's environment. Murie's classic study (1944) of the wolves of McKinley National Park was the first thorough examination of wolves on caribou ranges, and provides insight into how wolves switch their hunting between caribou and other prey such as moose and mountain sheep. Haber (1977) studied wolf packs of the same area in great detail twenty-five years later, and offers many suggestions about the relationship between wolves and their prey. Kuyt (1972) described the food habits and general ecology of wolves on the barren-ground caribou ranges of central Canada, and was the first to prove, by ear-tagging wolf pups, that the wolves migrated hundreds of miles twice each year following the caribou. Stephenson and James (in press) have made similar studies in northwestern Alaska. Miller (1975), Crisler (1956), and Burkholder (1959) have provided valuable observations of wolves' techniques of hunting caribou and their selection of prey. Rausch (1967) and Parker (1973) may be consulted for estimates of the size of wolf populations on some of the Alaskan and Canadian caribou ranges. Although the wolf is the major predator of the caribou, Reynolds (1980) has shown that grizzly bears can be effective predators of caribou calves within the calves' first three weeks of life, and Bergerud (1971) showed that lynx kill caribou calves in Newfoundland.

Bergerud (1980) reviewed the population dynamics of caribou, and has provided convincing evidence that predators control populations of barren-ground caribou, and that human hunting in conjunction with normal predator populations will cause declines in the size of caribou herds. Bergerud particularly rejects the idea that over-grazing of ranges or destruction of winter ranges by forest fires are responsible for caribou declines, a conclusion supported by Miller (1976) and Davis and Franzmann (1979). Bos (1975) and Davis, Valkenburg, and Reynolds (1980) have documented the decline of two large caribou herds in Alaska owing to overhunting. Calef (1974) and Geist (1978) discussed the potential effects of several types of northern development on the caribou, and Child (1973) reported the results of experiments on caribou crossing a simulated pipeline. Cameron and his co-workers have conducted research on the behaviour of the Central Arctic herd following the construction of the Trans-Alaska Pipeline System (Cameron et al., 1979; Cameron and Whitten, 1980).

The vital importance of the caribou to northern native peoples has been documented by many explorers, anthropologists, and archaeologists (Spiess, 1979). Burch (1972) has analyzed the lifestyle and hunting strategy that the caribou's migratory habits have imposed on hunting peoples. He clearly shows that caribou hunting societies are governed by the same ecological laws as other predators. Smith (1975) and Sharp (1977) have detailed the adaptations of the Chipewyan Indians to the life of hunting caribou, with special emphasis on the social organization that ensured the sharing of the kill among hunting bands. Birket-Smith (1929) recorded the central role of the caribou in the lives of the inland Eskimos of northern Canada. Although northern native peoples no longer depend exclusively on hunting, caribou meat still provides an important and highly valued source of food in many communities, and the people consider the right to hunt a basic part of their cultural identity (Berger, 1977; Interdisciplinary Systems Ltd., 1978).

Much still remains to be learned about the barren-ground caribou. A representative sample of the type of research now underway may be found in the *Proceedings of the Second International Reindeer/Caribou Symposium* (Reimers, Gaare, and Skjenneberg, eds., 1980). These proceedings also contain the most up-to-date published information on the population status of all major caribou and reindeer herds in the world.

Banfield, A.W.F. 1954. *Preliminary Investigation of the Barren-ground Caribou.* Department of Northern Affairs and National Resources, Canadian Wildlife Service, Wildlife Management Bulletin, Series 1, Nos. 10A and 10B. 79 pp. and 112 pp.

________. 1961. *A Revision of the Reindeer and Caribou, Genus* Rangifer. National Museums of Canada, Biological Series 66, Bulletin 177. 137 pp.

Berger, T.R. 1977. *Northern Frontier, Northern Homeland: The Report of the Mackenzie Valley Pipeline Inquiry.* Ottawa: Minister of Supply and Services Canada. 2 vols. 213 pp. and 268 pp.

Bergerud, A.T. 1971. *The Population Dynamics of Newfoundland Caribou.* Washington: The Wildlife Society, Wildlife Monograph No. 25. 55 pp.

________. 1974a. The role of the environment in the aggregation, movement and disturbance behaviour of caribou. In *The Behaviour of Ungulates and its Relation to Management,* ed. V. Geist and F. Walther, Vol. 2, pp. 552-584. The Papers of an International Symposium held at the University of Calgary, Alberta, Canada, 2-5 November 1971. Morges, Switzerland: International Union for Conservation of Nature and Natural Resources, IUCN Publications New Series No. 24.

________. 1974b. Rutting behaviour of Newfoundland caribou. In *The Behaviour of Ungulates and its Relation to Management,* ed. V. Geist and F. Walther, Vol. 1, pp. 395-435. The Papers of an International Symposium held at the University of Calgary, Alberta, Canada, 2-5 November 1971. Morges, Switzerland: International Union for Conservation of Nature and Natural Resources, IUCN Publications New Series No. 24.

________. 1980. A review of the population dynamics of caribou and wild reindeer in North America. In *Proceedings of the Second International Reindeer/Caribou Symposium, Røros, Norway, 1979,* ed. E. Reimers, E. Gaare, and S. Skjenneberg, pp. 556-581. Trondheim: Direktoratet for Vilt Og Ferskvannsfisk.

Best, G. 1938. *The Three Voyages of Martin Frobisher.* In Search of a Passage to Cathay and India by the North-West, A.D. 1576-8. From the original 1578 text by George Best, ed. V. Stefansson. London: Argonaut Press. 2 vols.

Birket-Smith, K. 1929. The Caribou Eskimos. Material and social life and their cultural position. 1. Descriptive part. In *Report of the Fifth Thule Expedition 1921-24,* Vol. 5. Copenhagen: Gyldeddalske Boghandel, Nordisk Forlag. 306 pp.

Bos, G.N. 1975. A partial analysis of the current population status of the Nelchina caribou herd. In *Proceedings of the First International Reindeer and Caribou Symposium, 9-11 August 1972, University of Alaska, Fairbanks, Alaska,* ed. J.R. Luick et al., pp. 170-180. Fairbanks: Biological Papers of the University of Alaska, Special Report No. 1.

Brown, G. B. 1928. *The Art of the Cave Dweller: A Study of the Earliest Artistic Activities of Man.* London: John Murray. 280 pp.

Burch, E.S., Jr. 1972. The caribou/wild reindeer as a human resource. *American Antiquity* 37(3): 339-368.

Burkholder, B.L. 1959. Movements and behavior of a wolf pack in Alaska. *Journal of Wildlife Management* 23(1): 1-11.

Calef, G.W. 1974. The predicted impact of the Canadian Arctic Gas pipeline project on the Porcupine caribou herd. In Research Reports, Vol. 4, of *Environmental Impact Assessment of the Portion of the Mackenzie Gas Pipeline from Alaska to Alberta,* pp. 101-120. Winnipeg: Environment Protection Board.

Cameron, R.D., and K.R. Whitten. 1980. Influence of the Trans-Alaska Pipeline corridor on the local disturbance of caribou. In *Proceedings of the Second International Reindeer/Caribou Symposium, Røros, Norway, 1979,* ed. E. Reimers, E. Gaare, and S. Skjenneberg, pp. 475-484. Trondheim: Direktoratet for Vilt Og Ferskvannsfisk.

Cameron, R.D. et al. 1979. Caribou distribution and group composition associated with construction of the Trans-Alaska Pipeline. *Canadian Field-Naturalist* 93(2): 155-162.

Child, K.N. 1973. *The Reactions of Barren-ground Caribou* (Rangifer tarandus granti) *to Simulated Pipeline and Pipeline Crossing Structures at Prudhoe Bay, Alaska.* Fairbanks: University of Alaska, Alaska Cooperative Wildlife Research Unit, Completion Report. 51 pp.

Clarke, C.H.D. 1940. *A Biological Investigation of the Thelon Game Sanctuary.* Ottawa: Department of Mines and Resources, Mines and Geology Branch, National Museum of Canada, Bulletin No. 96. 136 pp.

Crisler, L. 1956. Observations of wolves hunting caribou. *Journal of Mammalogy* 37(3): 337-346.

Curatolo, J.A. 1975. *Factors Influencing Local Movements and Behavior of Barren-ground Caribou* (Rangifer tarandus granti). Fairbanks: University of Alaska, M.Sc. thesis. 145 pp.

Dauphiné, T.C., Jr. 1976. *Biology of the Kaminuriak Population of Barren-ground Caribou. Part 4: Growth, reproduction and energy reserves.* Canadian Wildlife Service Report Series, No. 38. Ottawa: Minister of Supply and Services Canada. 71 pp.

Davis, J.L., and A.W. Franzmann, 1979. Fire-moose-caribou interrelationships: a review and assessment. In *Proceedings of the North American Moose Conference and Workshop,* Vol. 15, pp. 1-18. Soldotna-Kenai, Alaska.

_______, P. Valkenburg, and H.V. Reynolds. 1980. Population dynamics of Alaska's Western Arctic caribou herd. In *Proceedings of the Second International Reindeer /Caribou Symposium, Røros, Norway, 1979,* ed. E. Reimers, E. Gaare, and S. Skjenneberg, pp. 595-604. Trondheim: Direktoratet for Vilt Og Ferskvannsfisk.

Edwards, R.Y., and R.W. Ritcey. 1959. Migrations of caribou in a mountainous area in Wells Gray Park, British Columbia. *Canadian Field-Naturalist* 73(1): 21-25.

Franklin, J. 1823. *Narrative of a Journey to the Shores of the Polar Sea in the Years 1819, 20, 21, and 22.* London: John Murray. 768 pp.

Geist, V. 1978. Behaviour. Chapter 19 in *Big Game of North America,* ed. J.L. Schmidt and D.L. Gilbert, pp. 283-296. Harrisburg, Pa.: Wildlife Management Institute, Stackpole Books.

Haber, G.C. 1977. *Socio-ecological Dynamics of Wolves and Prey in a Sub-arctic Ecosystem.* Vancouver: University of British Columbia, Ph.D. thesis.

Hearne, S. 1795. *A Journey from Prince of Wales's Fort in Hudson's Bay to the Northern Ocean 1769, 1770, 1771, 1772.* London: A. Strahan and T. Cadell.

Henshaw, J. 1968. The activities of wintering caribou in northwestern Alaska in relation to weather and snow conditions. *International Journal of Biometeorology* 12 (1): 21-27.

Interdisciplinary Systems Ltd. 1978. *Effects of Exploration and Development in the Baker Lake Area,* Vol. 1. Prepared for the Department of Indian Affairs and Northern Development. Winnipeg.

Kelsall, J.P. 1968. *The Migratory Barren-ground Caribou of Canada.* Ottawa: Queen's Printer. 340 pp.

Kuyt, E. 1972. *Food Habits and Ecology of Wolves on Barren-ground Caribou Range in the Northwest Territories.* Canadian Wildlife Service Report Series, No. 21. Ottawa: Information Canada. 36 pp.

LaPerriere, A.J., and P.C. Lent. 1977. Caribou feeding sites in relation to snow characteristics in northeastern Alaska. *Arctic* 30(2): 101-108.

Lent, P.C. 1965. Rutting behaviour in a barren-ground caribou population. *Animal Behaviour* 13(2-3): 259-264.

_______. 1966. Calving and related social behavior in the barren-ground caribou. *Zeitschrift für Tierpsychologie* 23(6): 701-756.

Lommel, A. 1966. *Prehistoric and Primitive Man.* New York: Paul Hamlyn.

Miller, D.R. 1975. Observations of wolf predation on barren ground caribou in winter. In *Proceedings of the First International Reindeer and Caribou Symposium, 9-11 August 1972, University of Alaska, Fairbanks, Alaska,* ed. J.R. Luick et al., pp. 209-220. Fairbanks: Biological Papers of the University of Alaska, Special Report No. 1.

_______. 1976. *Wildfire and Caribou on the Taiga Ecosystem of Northcentral Canada.* Moscow, Idaho: University of Idaho, Ph.D. thesis. 131 pp.

Miller, F.L. 1974. *Biology of the Kaminuriak Population of Barren-ground caribou. Part 2: Dentition as an indicator of age and sex; composition and socialization of the population.* Canadian Wildlife Service Report Series, No. 31. Ottawa: Information Canada. 88 pp.

_______ et al. 1975. Distribution, movements and socialization of barren ground caribou radio-tracked on their calving and post-calving areas. In *Proceedings of the First International Reindeer and Caribou Symposium, 9-11 August 1972, University of Alaska, Fairbanks, Alaska,* ed. J.R. Luick et al., pp. 423-435. Fairbanks: Biological Papers of the University of Alaska, Special Report No. 1.

Moulin, R.J. 1965. *Prehistoric Painting.* New York: Funk and Wagnalls. 207 pp.

Murie, A. 1944. *The Wolves of Mount McKinley.* U.S. Department of the Interior, National Park Service, Fauna Series No. 5. 238 pp.

Murie, O.J. 1935. *Alaska-Yukon Caribou.* United States Department of Agriculture, Bureau of Biological Survey, North American Fauna No. 54. Washington, D.C. 93 pp.

Neiland, K.A., and C. Dukeminier. 1972. *A Bibliography of the Parasites, Diseases, and Disorders of Several Important Wild Ruminants of the Northern Hemisphere.* Juneau: Alaska Department of Fish and Game, Game Technical Bulletin No. 3. 151 pp.

Parker, G.R. 1973. Distribution and densities of wolves within barren-ground caribou range in northern mainland Canada. *Journal of Mammalogy* 54(2): 341-348.

Pike, W. 1892. *The Barren Ground of Northern Canada.* New York: Macmillan. 300 pp.

Powell, T.G.E. 1966. *Prehistoric Art.* New York: Frederick A. Praeger. 284 pp.

Pruitt, W.O., Jr. 1959. Snow as a factor in the winter ecology of the barren ground caribou *(Rangifer arcticus). Arctic* 12(3): 158-179.

_______. 1960. *Behavior of the Barren-ground Caribou.* Fairbanks: Biological Papers of the University of Alaska, No. 3. 44 pp.

Rausch, R.A. 1967. Some aspects of the population ecology of wolves, Alaska. *American Zoologist* 7(2): 253-265.

Reimers, E., E. Gaare, and S. Skjenneberg, eds. 1980. *Proceedings of the Second International Reindeer / Caribou Symposium, Røros, Norway, 1979.* Trondheim: Direktoratet for Vilt Og Ferskvannsfisk. 799 pp.

Reynolds, H.V. 1980. *North Slope Grizzly Bear Studies.* Juneau: Alaska Department of Fish and Game, Federal Aid in Wildlife Restoration Project W-17-11. 75 pp.

Richardson, J. 1829. *Fauna Boreali-Americana; or the Zoology of the Northern Parts of British America.* Pt. 1, Mammalia. London: John Murray. 300 pp.

Roby, D.D. 1978. *Behavioral Patterns of Barren-ground Caribou of the Central Arctic Herd Adjacent to the Trans-Alaska Oil Pipeline.* Fairbanks: University of Alaska, M.Sc. thesis. 200 pp.

Scott, R.F., E.F. Chatelain, and W.A. Elkins. 1950. The status of the Dall sheep and caribou in Alaska. In *North American Wildlife Conference Transactions,* Vol. 15, pp. 612-626. Washington: Wildlife Management Institute.

Sharp, H.S. 1977. The caribou-eater Chipewyan: bilaterality, strategies of caribou hunting, and the fur trade. *Arctic Anthropology* 14(2): 35-40.

Shea, J.C. 1978. *Social Behavior of Wintering Caribou in Northwestern Alaska.* Fairbanks: University of Alaska, M.Sc. thesis. 112 pp.

Sieveking, A. 1979. *The Cave Artists.* London: Thames and Hudson. 221 pp.

Skoog, R.O. 1968. *Ecology of the Caribou* (Rangifer tarandus granti) *in Alaska.* Berkeley: University of California, Ph.D. thesis. 699 pp.

Smith, J.G.E. 1975. The ecological basis of Chipewyan socio-territorial organization. In *Proceedings of the Northern Athapaskan Conference, 1971,* ed. A. McF. Clark, Vol. 2, pp. 389-461. Ottawa: National Museum of Man Mercury Series, Canadian Ethnology Service Paper No. 27.

Spiess, A.E. 1979. *Reindeer and Caribou Hunters.* New York: Academic Press. 312 pp.

Stardom, R.R.P. 1975. Woodland caribou and snow conditions in southeast Manitoba. In *Proceedings of the First International Reindeer and Caribou Symposium, 9-11 August 1972, University of Alaska, Fairbanks, Alaska,* ed. J.R. Luick et al., pp. 324-334. Fairbanks: Biological Papers of the University of Alaska, Special Report No. 1.

Stefansson, V. 1913. *My Life with the Eskimo.* New York: Macmillan. 538 pp.

Stephenson, R.O., and D.A. James. In press. A preliminary report on wolf movements and food habits in northwestern Alaska. In *Proceedings of the Portland Wolf Symposium, Portland, Oregon, 1979.*

Thing, H. 1977. *Behavior, Mechanics and Energetics associated with Winter Cratering by Caribou in Northwestern Alaska.* Fairbanks: Biological Papers of the University of Alaska, No. 18. 41 pp.

Design by Howard Pain
Typesetting by Shervill-Dickson Limited
Film separations and printing by Herzig Somerville Limited
Binding by The Bryant Press Limited
Printed and bound in Canada